# Fragrant Designs

Beth Hanson
Editor

Elizabeth Peters
DIRECTOR OF
PUBLICATIONS

Sigrun Wolff Saphire
SENIOR EDITOR

Gerry Moore
SCIENCE EDITOR

Joni Blackburn
COPY EDITOR

Elizabeth Ennis
ART DIRECTOR

Scot Medbury
PRESIDENT

Elizabeth Scholtz
DIRECTOR
EMERITUS

Handbook #193

Copyright © 2009 by Brooklyn Botanic Garden, Inc.

All-Region Guides are published by Brooklyn Botanic
Garden, 1000 Washington Ave., Brooklyn, NY 11225.

Subscription included in Brooklyn Botanic Garden
subscriber membership dues (bbg.org/subscribe).

ISBN 13: 978-1-889538-47-1
ISBN 10: 1-889538-47-7

Printed by OGP in China.
♻ Printed with soy-based ink on
100% postconsumer recycled paper.

Delight insect pollinators and human visitors alike by planting scented flowers and other
fragrant plants, such as the flowering tobacco and dill on the cover and the sweet rudbeckia
(*Rudbeckia submentosa* 'Henry Eilers'), above.

# Fragrant Designs

# Fragrance: A Sensual Science

## Beth Hanson

Plants send messages to animals ("Sweet nectar here!" "My leaves are toxic!") and to other plants ("Predator Alert!") encoded in many of the same chemicals that make fragrant plants appealing to humans. We have used these scents for our own ends for eons—as medicines, perfumes, spices, cleaning agents, and to create fragrant gardens. As gardeners we spend a lot of time around plants. By learning how they evolved along with their surroundings and how they use scents to function and communicate, we develop a deeper understanding of the rich relationships among plants and animals. We can create natural havens that give us the opportunity to observe, up close, inter-actions between fragrant plants and their pollinators and predators. At the same time, we can use scent to create inviting spots for ourselves and for our family and friends.

In this book, BBG's own gardeners and talented horticulturists from other public gardens show you how to put together delicious-smelling gardens. Fragrance is the focus, but looks don't take a backseat in the eight projects featured here. The evening garden is at its fragrant peak at night, and the light-colored flowers and foliage glow in the moonlight as the plants' scents lure their moth pollinators. Three gorgeous con-tainers bring the aromas of the Mediterranean, Southeast Asian cuisine, and a country dooryard to your terrace, or any other place that you'd like to enrich with yummy scents. The garden of fragrant natives is a layered, naturalistic woodland where local wildlife species will feel right at home. Scented shrubs, perennials, annuals, and vines transform a path, hell strip, front garden, and back patio into vibrant, perfumed spots. In a garden designed especially for children, kids can explore, have fun, and learn, gaining hands-on gardening experience along the way. And the most famous scented plant, the rose, is the star of its own garden, surrounded by other plants that enhance its beauty and perfume.

Each project's author has selected an array of great-smelling plants that blend together into an inspiring design—rendered in a watercolor illustration in the book and accompanied by an online portfolio that includes a detailed scale planting plan. (Find it at bbg.org/fragrantdesigns.) Use the gardens in this book as a starting-off point or follow the suggestions of the authors. Either way, you'll welcome the handy tips for planting and maintaining the wonderfully fragrant plants you choose.

**Draw human and animal visitors to your garden with an offering of fabulous scents.**

# Making Sense of Scents

**Beth Hanson**

Scientists have recently uncovered lots of clues as to how our senses—especially our sense of smell—work. In the field of functional genomics, they are decoding our genes for scent receptors, and in cognitive science, we are learning which parts of the brain are involved in scent recognition. In the world of plant science, new findings are showing how plants use scents to communicate, overturning the notion of plants as passive beings. We now know that plants participate in complex "conversations" with pollinators and other animals—even with other plants—using the volatile chemicals they release. But what does all this science have to do with gardeners? Humans may not be the primary targets of plant scents, but we have long applied our ingenuity to turning these scents, or rather the chemical compounds that are responsible for them, to our own uses—as medicines, perfumes, preservatives, and flavorings, and often simply for pleasure, the kind of sensual enjoyment you come to discover in a fragrance garden.

While our sense of smell is not as acute as that of some other mammals, it is fundamental to our health and well-being. Smell is intimately linked to our ability to taste food—and it helps us detect dangers that may lurk there. In subconscious ways smell may help us choose a mate. It prods and stirs our memories and is at the root of all kinds of pleasurable and unpleasant sensations. Through advances in the science of smell we are learning more about what happens in our noses and brains when we encounter an aroma. Interest in this area of research is high—in fact, a 2004 Nobel Prize went to two scientists for work showing how the brain organizes information it receives through the nose.

New tools and techniques have enabled scientists to fill in many of the details of olfaction. Researchers in the field of functional genomics have begun identifying specific odor receptors in the nose. Using functional MRI—an imaging test that allows us to see what parts of the brain are stimulated during different activities—neuroscientists can study the brain as it responds to and registers a smell. With gas chromatography and mass spectrometry we have better ways of analyzing smells in the real world and breaking them down into their minutest components. In the sidebar "Scent Seeker," on page 10, learn how the chemist and botanist Roman Kaiser has spent the past 30 years tracking down plants and teasing apart the chemical components of their scents.

The 40 million or so olfactory receptor neurons in a human nose help us make sense of the smells around us, including the heady scent wafting up from the lavender in this garden.

Olfaction—the act of smelling—is complex. Here's what we now know: As you move through the world, on a stroll through the garden, perhaps, you encounter an array of scents at every step. Among these, you recognize, say, thyme (*Thymus vulgaris*) broadcasting an aromatic message. The scent of thyme's foliage, or its aromatic profile, is composed of more than 30 volatile chemicals, so light they float on the breeze. Most of these chemicals are present in trace amounts, but a few of them—thymol, gamma-terpinene, rho-cymene, linalool, myrcene, alpha-pinene, and alpha-thujene—dominate.

You breathe in—perhaps sniffing to concentrate the scents—and the molecules flow into your nostrils, passing up through the convoluted passageway in the nasal cavity to the olfactory cleft and past a dime-sized patch of tissue under the eye sockets. This tissue—the olfactory epithelium—is studded with 40 million or so olfactory receptor neurons. From the tip of each of these neurons, many tiny, hairlike cilia protrude into the mucus membrane that covers the epithelium. These cilia are coated with olfactory receptors, which can bind, with more or less affinity, to a variety of odor molecules.

As the thyme scent wafts up your nose, some of the aromatic molecules bind with receptors. Once a certain number of molecules are bound, the neurons send an electrical signal along nerve fibers (axons) that pass through a sievelike bone called the cribriform plate to the olfactory bulb of the brain. The information is sorted and categorized here, then travels to the limbic system, a set of brain structures (including the amygdala and hippocampus) at the top of the brain stem and below the cortex. The limbic system is central to our emotions and motivations, especially those related to survival. This is where memories, emotions, and odors converge, and some people believe that this confluence explains why smell is often a trigger for vivid memories and potent emotions.

The Nobel Prize winners Richard Axel and Linda B. Buck discovered how mammals make sense of smells: Specific combinations of olfactory receptors, not individual receptors, as one might expect, perceive distinct smells. Most odors are "elaborate bouquets, mixtures of dozens if not hundreds of molecules," writes smell scientist Avery Gilbert in his book *What the Nose Knows*. Our brains perceive these mixtures as distinct odorant patterns, analogous to the combinations of different instruments in a symphony. When the electrical signals triggered by thyme eventually make their way to the cortex, their final destination in the brain, you think, "Aha! Thyme!"

Humans may all process smells in the same manner (Axel and Buck discovered that sensory maps in the olfactory areas of the brain are identical from person to person), but people experience the same odor in very different ways. Some people are very aware of specific smells that to others are not noticeable. There is also tremendous variation in how much people like or dislike specific scents. Scientists recently showed that seemingly small variations in the genes that encode odor receptors help explain why different people describe the same smell as offensive, pleasant, or undetectable.

**Flower scents' primary targets are pollinators such as this sphinx moth, but luckily for us, the fragrances of many flowers are just as appealing to human noses.**

Place a fragrant plant next to a path and note how the scent of the flowers or aromatic foliage affects the mood of those who pass near enough to breath it in.

Social scientists point out that cultural influences also play a big part in how people react to particular smells.

Men and women are not equal when it comes to the ability to smell. "Women detect odors at lower concentrations and are better able to identify them by name," writes Gilbert. The anthropologist Lionel Tiger speculates that this difference may be due to women's role during our lengthy evolutionary phase as hunter-gatherers. Women were responsible for gathering fruits and vegetables, and they relied on their sense of smell to judge the ripeness and safety of these foods.

It is becoming clear, too, that expectation and suggestion are very important to people's perception of smell. In a recent experiment, the subjects were told that lavender had relaxing properties, and when their heart rates and skin conductance were measured, they had indeed relaxed. Another group was told that lavender was stimulating, and using the same measurements, researchers found that to the members of this group, it was indeed stimulating.

A fragrance garden is a perfect laboratory to test your own sensations and expectations. Fill it with potent-smelling plants and take note of how you and others react to specific scents. Observe the goings-on between the plants and animals, and you may pick up some of their animated chemical conversation. "The scents of nature are largely a chemical conversation between plants and animals," writes Gilbert, "and humans merely eavesdrop."

# SCENT SEEKER: ROMAN KAISER

Like putting together a jigsaw puzzle, the human brain assembles the distinct chemical parts of a scent into a coherent pattern that it can recognize and remember. Roman Kaiser's quest has been to find entrancing smells, then take them apart and identify the components. Kaiser, a chemist, botanist, and perfumer at the Swiss flavor and fragrance company Givaudan, has traveled the globe for the past 40 years—visiting rainforests, mountainsides, and seacoasts—in search of new scent molecules.

In the 1970s, Kaiser and his colleagues developed a technique to collect the fragrant exhalations of living plants. Unlike perfumers' traditional techniques in which flowers are destroyed in the process of gathering their essences, Kaiser collects scents from living flowers and plants. To do this, he harmlessly encloses an entire flower, root, leaf, or fruit in a glass bulb for an hour or so and captures the plant's volatile molecules in a porous material like charcoal. He then dissolves these molecules in a solvent and, using gas chromatography, separates them into their chemical components. Finally, he identifies these chemicals using a technique called mass spectrometry. Kaiser has determined the aromatic profile—the recipe that makes up a particular smell—of nearly 2,500 plant scents with this method.

Along the way, Kaiser discovered that certain volatile chemicals occur frequently in scented plants. Among them are linalool, which has a tender sweet smell; beta-

ionone, which gives violets and yellow freesia their distinctive smell; aromatic compounds, such as phenylethyl alcohol, which also have a sweet aspect and are central to rose scents; and lipid-derived volatiles (cis-3-hexanol), which give plant scents their leafy, grassy, "green" notes.

Kaiser has investigated entire "smellscapes" or olfactory sceneries, the characteristic aromas of specific places, among them a forest biotope in Sequoia National Park and a tobacconist's shop. In the process, Kaiser and his team

**This apparatus captures and analyzes fragrance molecules emanating from the flower.**

*Laelia gouldiana*, an orchid presumed extinct in the wild, is an olfactory delight, with a floral scent rounded out by violetlike and tender woody notes, says Roman Kaiser.

also track down individual scents. For example, on one field trip, they traced a "transparent, resinous, woody, musky scent" on a Mediterranean coastal hillside to its source in a nearby forest. They found that the scent came from the resin of the maritime pine, *Pinus pinaster*, when it was exposed to sunshine. By identifying the main scent-contributing building blocks of a smellscape, Kaiser can then recombine the scents in his lab to re-create an olfactory image of that landscape.

Kaiser's travels are now directed toward what he says is his final large project: capturing and documenting the fragrances of rare and endangered plants before they vanish. Many plants facing extinction are found in the rainforest. No surprise, says Kaiser, since 80 percent of the earth's plant and animal species are found there. On one trip to the rainforest in French Guyana, Kaiser and his team explored the treetop canopy from small airships. "The rainforest treetop region is especially interesting because it is the most life-intensive biosphere of all. Exploring it is the dream of botanists, biologists, and of course, scent researchers," says Kaiser.

Botanists believe that human activities are causing the extinction of five plant species every day, Kaiser says. "Most have never been recognized, much less classified or analyzed. What has happened to the human spirit that so much of the basic stuff of life is so threatened today?"

# Capturing Scent
## Leda Meredith

Since frankincense was first burnt on charcoal thousands of years ago, people have explored ingenious ways to overcome the ephemeral nature of plant fragrances and keep them within nose's reach at all times. These days the popularity of aromatherapy is testament to the ancient idea that scents influence our physical and mental well-being. What follows is a brief overview of a few basic methods developed over the ages to capture plant scents and release them at will.

**Incense** Derived from the Latin verb *incendere*, meaning "to set on fire," incense describes a substance that gives off a fragrant scent when burned. Traditionally, tree resins like frankincense (*Boswellia* species), barks such as cinnamon, and aromatic woods such as sandalwood are made into incense, usually because it is the easiest method to extract their fragrance.

**Infused Oils** These are made by loosely packing a vessel with fresh or dried plant material, covering it with a vegetable oil or melted animal fat, and leaving the oil to infuse for four to six weeks. The plants impart their scent to the carrier oil and are then strained out. Across northern Africa and throughout the Mediterranean, olive, sesame, and other oils were infused with fragrant plants using this technique quite possibly as long as 9,000 years ago. As far as we know, all the scented products used up until the first century were burned as incense or infused in fats, water (to scent baths), or wine (to impart flavor as well as aroma).

**Steam Distillation of Essential Oils** Unlike infused oils, essential oils are highly concentrated: It can take up to 4,000 pounds of rose petals to make one pound of rose oil, or attar of rose, by steam distillation. To derive a plant's essential oil, large quantities of plant material are placed in the chamber of a still, and a flow of steam is introduced. The steam releases the essential oils from the plant material and carries them out of the chamber and into a chilled condenser. The cooling process turns the steam back into a liquid. The essential oils separate from the water and are then collected.

The first written record of steam distillation is found in an Alexandrian text, describing a still invented by the first-century alchemist Maria Prophetissima. Today, essential oils are used in the perfume industry and in aromatherapy.

**Enfleurage** In this process, developed in France in the 19th century, batch upon batch of fresh flower petals are pressed between glass sheets in a neutral fat that is solid at room temperature, like pork fat or beef tallow. Once the fat has taken on the scent of the flowers, the plant residue is removed and wax is added to produce a pomade. Enfleurage is a more costly process than distillation and nowadays is only used for a few essential oils, such as those of tuberoses and jasmine.

**Absolute** Some flowers are too delicate for steam distillation or contain fragrance molecules that cannot be completely released by water. In addition to the enfleurage method, their aroma can also be captured in an absolute. To make an absolute, the flowers are first exposed to an organic solvent (such as hexane). This results in a semisolid mixture of plant wax and volatile oils known as a concrete, which is then processed in ethyl alcohol. The volatile plant oils separate from the wax into the alcohol, and the alcohol is then evaporated. What is left is the absolute. Jasmine and rose oils are frequently extracted by this method.

**Perfume** Though the dictionary definition describes perfume simply as a fragrant liquid used to impart a pleasant smell to one's body or clothes, in the modern fragrance industry, a perfume is the most concentrated and expensive scent made. Eau de parfum, eau de toilette, and eau de cologne are less costly dilutions of a perfume. Today's perfumes typically include both plant extractions, such as essential oils, and synthetic scents blended in a carrier base of either a neutral fatty oil or ethyl alcohol.

Most perfumes include a top note, middle note, and base note. The top note is the most volatile scent—the first smell you are aware of when you inhale. It evaporates quickly. Lavender is an example of a top note. The middle note evaporates more slowly and serves to harmonize the top note and the base note. Clary sage is an example of a frequently used middle note. The base note is the scent that lingers longest, well after the top and middle notes have evaporated. It is usually an earthy scent, commonly derived from patchouli leaves, vetiver root, or a fragrant wood like sandalwood.

**Synonymous with delicious scents, the oil from rose petals has been a staple of the fragrance industry for many centuries.**

Lured by its subtle scent, a virescent green metallic bee visits a coneflower in search of a supply of nutritious nectar and pollen.

# Perfume for Pollinators

Janet Marinelli

And we think we invented scratch 'n' sniff, perfume strips, and other forms of olfactory advertising. The truth is, plants beat us to it by at least a hundred million years. Plants advertise with fragrance in various ways. For example, they perfume their blooms to seduce the insects, bats, and other critters they need to pollinate their flowers. Floral fragrance is a kind of olfactory come-on that proclaims to a potential flower fertilizer, "Come hither, honey, 'cause there's scrumptious pollen and sweet nectar hidden inside these pretty petals." In addition to a full belly, the pollinator leaves with pollen attached to its body in a bundle or dusted on its fur. When the pollinator lands on another flower while looking for its next meal, cross-fertilization can occur.

Scientists believe that one reason plants are in big trouble around the globe is because their pollinators are disappearing. A major factor in their decline is loss of habitat to farms and urban development. Without their pollinators, the flowers of many species don't get fertilized. If they don't get fertilized, they don't set seed and can't reproduce. In a pinch, some plants can pollinate themselves, but this often causes inbreeding and other genetic problems that ultimately threaten the species' survival. By creating gardens that feature a variety of fragrant flowers to attract a diversity of pollinators, we gardeners can help compensate for the loss of habitat and lend plants and their partners a helping hand—and as a bonus get whiffs of heady scent ourselves.

## Signature Scents

Plants employ not just scent but also visual cues like flower color to facilitate reproduction. But it appears that during the early days of floral evolution, fragrance, not color, was the principal allure. Beetles were the most evolved insects during the late Jurassic and early Cretaceous periods, when flowering plants first appear. Although these primeval pollinators are virtually colorblind, they have a great sense of smell, so it's no big surprise that the magnolias and other primitive flowers they still pollinate today pack powerful perfumes.

Floral fragrance is far from an antiquated trait, however. Even the most highly evolved flowers, such as orchids, use it to captivate their reproductive partners. In fact, although flowers can be identical in color and shape, no two floral fragrances are alike. Every plant has its own signature scent, a complex mixture of volatile organic compounds that easily turn to gases and waft through the air. Some 1,700 compounds have been identified in flower fragrances so far, according to Natalia Dudareva, a molecular biologist at Purdue University, whose specialty is floral scents. An orchid can produce a hundred different volatile compounds, she points out, while a snapdragon produces seven to ten.

Dudareva recently isolated the gene for one of these compounds, methyl benzoate. Some 30 to 40 commercially important plants—including snapdragons, flowering tobaccos, and petunias—use this same fragrance-generation system. Intensive breeding for bigger, more colorful blooms during the past decades evidently has deactivated the gene, which is why so many recent cultivars are disappointing in the scent department. A plant that is pouring so much energy into producing flashier-looking flowers, Dudareva hypothesizes, is in essence too pooped to make perfume.

To date, little is known about how pollinators respond to the individual compounds found in flower scents. But it is clear that they are capable of distinguishing among complex scent mixtures and therefore among plant species—their schnozzolas steer them to the ones that provide the most delectable nectar or pollen. Hence, over the eons, plants have evolved floral fragrances that best cater to the olfactory proclivities of their most efficient pollinators.

You could say that it's all in the proboscis of the beholder (or antennae, the olfactory organs of bees, beetles, and moths). Pollinators are very picky about flower odors. Bees, for example, prefer the sweet scent of plants like snapdragons and sweet peas. Beetles are partial to flowers with fruity and spicy scents, such as magnolias.

Moths, which are mostly nocturnal, are attracted to flowers such as jasmine, which advertise their presence under the cloak of darkness with strong, sweet perfumes. Moths have a keen sense of smell and have even been known to pick up the

scent of an enticing plant from 900 feet away. Bats are also night flyers with good noses, but they favor blooms with musty aromas.

Within the various groups of flower fertilizers there are generalists, which have cosmopolitan floral tastes, and specialists, which have a monogamous relationship with the blossoms they visit. Among the ultimate pollinator specialists are the moths that fertilize yuccas. Yuccas, including about 30 species native to North America, such as Spanish bayonet and Joshua tree, typically send up stout stalks of white flowers, which are pollinated only by yucca moths. And 70 percent of yucca moth species visit the flowers of only one particular yucca species.

**Jack-in-the-pulpit perfumes its flower with the scent of rotten fish, which attracts its fly pollinators.**

## False Advertising

Pollinators aren't always too bright about using fragrance to find the flowers that offer the best rewards, and some flowers exploit their gullibility by resorting to false advertising. Consider jack-in-the-pulpit, skunk cabbage, and other aroids, whose tiny flowers, massed together along a fleshy pole partially surrounded by a leaf, smell of stinking fish and feces. Flies arrive with great expectations of finding some rotting tissue in which to lay their eggs. They get trapped inside a chamber at the base of the leaf that protects the fertile flowers and remain incarcerated until the flowering pole wilts. In the process of trying to escape, they pollinate the plant.

False or not, when it comes to advertising scent, timing is everything. Different flowers flaunt their fragrance at different times. According to Dudareva, snapdragons release four times more scent during the day, when their bee pollinators are busy foraging, than at night. By contrast, nicotianas are most fragrant after dusk, when their moth pollinators are out and about. What's more, flowers show off their perfumes only when they are good and ready for fertilization. Newly opened blossoms don't produce as much scent as mature ones do, and fertilized flowers make less—and less enticing—perfume.

# AIR POLLUTION "SILENCES" FRAGRANT PLANTS

## BETH HANSON

Plants can communicate in ways we are just beginning to understand, but these days plants in heavily populated areas are struggling to get their message out. A study by the University of Virginia has shown that common pollutants from power plants and cars, including ozone, hydroxyl, and nitrate radicals, rapidly bind with flower scent molecules. Once these molecules are bound together, the flower aroma is diminished or destroyed.

Before the industrial revolution, scent molecules produced by a flower could travel as far as 3,300 to 4,000 feet. In today's degraded environments near major cites, these molecules may travel only 660 to 985 feet before they bind to a pollutant and become scentless, according to José D. Fuentes, a professor of environmental sciences at the university and a coauthor of the study. In the most heavily polluted areas, flower aromas may be diminished by as much as 90 percent from the time before automobiles and heavy industry became widespread.

The dire conclusion of the study: Pollution has made it increasingly difficult for flowers to lure their pollinators, which may lead to decreased pollination rates. The effects of air pollution may be greatest on plants dependent on "specialist pollinators," because plant fragrances become less specific in polluted air, and plant fragrances tend to blur, creating a generic smell. "What was a unique signal in the 1800s has become a general signal," Fuentes reported.

Landscape fragmentation may aggravate the situation further for flowering plants and their pollinators, which rely on scent to locate isolated flower patches beyond their line of sight. The insects may end up spending more time searching for pollen sources and less time foraging. Less foraging means less pollen is moved and fewer flowers (and fruit) develop, a losing proposition all around.

**Air pollution makes it difficult for pollinators like the green scarab beetle to locate flowers.**

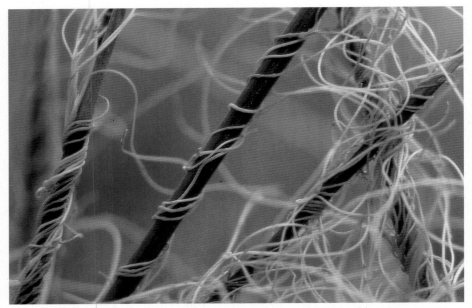

Dodder, a parasitic plant, stalks its plant victims by following their scent and then twining around their stems, absorbing water and nutrients.

# Mixed Messages

## Beth Hanson

A flower's perfume entices pollinators, which are essential to complete the plant's reproductive cycle. Fragrant essential oils in leaves, stems, bark, roots, and even woody parts contain different chemical compounds and send very different messages. Plants emit these scents when they are grazed, chewed, or trampled, and the aromatic signal, in these cases, means "scram!" To our noses, many of these plant scents are lovely, but to animal predators they serve as warnings, for when ingested, the fragrant compounds are sometimes toxic.

Floral scents are usually produced in relatively complex glands in flowers, while leaves seem to lack special odor-producing structures. The scents that leaves do produce are for the most part simpler molecules that have lower molecular weights than those of flower scents. These compounds are strongly antiseptic, since part of their role is to protect against diseases, and their scents tend to be more pungent, bitter, or medicinal than floral—think of eucalyptus, clove, and thyme foliage.

Such scents warn plant predators away, but they also attract the predators of the plant's pests—following "the enemy of my enemy is my friend" logic. They let other animals know that a plant predator such as a leaf-eating caterpillar is at work—and is available as food. When spider mites begin to chew on the leaves of lima bean vines, for example, the plants secrete a blend of volatile chemicals that attract other, predatory, mite species—ones that feast on spider mites.

Plant scents encode messages that animals understand, but scientists are discovering that other plants respond to these airborne missives as well. When a plant is under attack, the aromatic substances it releases act as a signal to nearby members of the same species. These neighbors rapidly produce enzymes that make their own leaves less palatable to herbivores. The aforementioned lima bean plants become less attractive to spider mites and more attractive to predatory wasps after downwind exposure to plants already infested by the mites. The healthy plants detect the signals from the infested plants upwind and are primed to respond more strongly to subsequent attacks.

Another kind of communication between plants is less beneficial to the signal-sender. Dodder (*Cuscuta* species), a parasitic plant that preys on a variety of wild and cultivated plants, finds its prey by following the scents these plants release, then twines itself around its target, absorbing water, minerals, and carbohydrates from its host.

Plant fragrances have many other functions. Many plants with aromatic foliage originated in hot, arid climates. The essential oils found in their leaves protect them from drought by forming a protective coating, preventing moisture from evaporating. If air temperatures are high enough, the walls of a plant's scent glands crack open, releasing their essential oils onto the leaf surfaces and into the air. Just walk through a eucalyptus grove or an herb garden on a hot summer afternoon and you will be able to smell this response to heat.

## WHAT'S THAT SMELL?

Nonflower scents are sometimes categorized into four main groups: those that smell like turpentine (for example, rosemary); camphor and eucalyptus (sages, catmint, scented geraniums); mint (mint family members); and sulfur (mustard, onions, garlic). The bark and roots of trees and shrubs are often turpenty. The roots of herbaceous perennials frequently have a flowery smell, such as the rose scent of some stonecrops (*Rhodiola rosea*) or violet scent of some iris roots (*Iris germanica, I. florentina,* and *I. pallida*).

**To protect against drying out on hot, dry days, the leaves of scented geranium release an oil, making their odor more pronounced.**

# Scented Gardens

Fragrance is the central theme of the lovely gardens portrayed on the following pages. As documented by the accompanying watercolor illustrations, each one of them offers a richly layered landscape that beckons with wonderful scents and sights from spring to fall. As lavish as each design appears with its offerings of fragrances, colors, and textures, it is stingy when it comes to the gardener's expense of time, labor, and money. Each garden is easy to install and maintain, requiring a mere dozen carefully chosen fragrant plants. (Printer-friendly plans and plant lists are available online at bbg.org/fragrantdesigns to make planning and planting a breeze.) Project-specific design and cultivation tips offer nifty ideas and practical advice that will come in handy when you are adapting a design to fit a particular site or are looking for inspiration to enrich the sensory experience of an existing garden with a few carefully placed scented annuals, perennials, shrubs, and vines. For example, think of an aromatic arbor over an inviting garden seat or a profusion of lavender blooming next to a hammock.

The more than 100 plants gathered here take you on a whirlwind tour of some of nature's most compelling flower and foliage scents. Front and center is an intoxicating bouquet of floral fragrances, some potent, some subtle, some at their most aromatic under the midday sun, others only perceptible at night. Flowers release their scents into the air to lure their pollinators and so advertise their presence without prompting. Scented foliage plants require direct contact: Leaves usually need to be brushed or lightly crushed to release their scents. The essential oils in the leaves are not there to attract pollinators but to discourage animals from eating them, which is why their scents aren't released until they are touched. Fragrant foliage may be more subtle overall, but the scents have staying power and are around whenever there are leaves on the plant. As you pick the stars and supporting cast of your fragrant garden, be sure to smell the flower and foliage fragrances so that you can be certain that your nose appreciates the plants as much as your eye.

Grow scented plants where their fragrances may be readily appreciated. Place flowers that release their fragrances after dark on a patio where you enjoy sitting with friends in the evening, or just outside a window that is left open on mild nights. If the leaves are the most fragrant part of the plant, grow them alongside paths or near borders where people can brush past them and enjoy their fragrance.

For an updated map of the USDA hardiness zones that reflects recent climate changes, visit the Arbor Day Foundation site at arborday.org/media/zones.cfm.

**Plant an entire garden, or start with a few fragrant plants like lavender, to delight pollinators and human visitors alike.**

# Fragrant Front Yard Gardens
## Meghan Ray

The front garden is our most visible opportunity to contribute to the landscape of the community. It is here we welcome friends and neighbors, and its setting gives us the chance to bring color, fragrance, and wildlife into our neighborhood. A front yard can be empty and sterile, especially when it is not used as the main family entrance, but an aromatic border that includes architectural shrubs, culinary herbs, and good cut flowers helps bring it to life. A bright, sunny garden buzzing with bees and butterflies and filled with wonderful-smelling herbs and flowers invites us to revisit the front of the house and spend some time there.

The following pages feature a design for a fragrant front yard garden that showcases flowering shrubs, prairie and meadow flowers, and culinary herbs. Together these provide flower and leaf fragrance; habitats for bees, butterflies, and birds; and continual visual interest. The design incorporates plants that flower from the late winter through autumn, offering an almost yearlong pollinator smorgasboard. This garden features spicy fragrances, with an emphasis on clove and lemon, and includes the tart, tannic foliage scents of members of the mint family like culinary sage (*Salvia officinalis*), thyme (*Thymus vulgaris*), and wormwood (*Artemisia* 'Powis Castle').

The garden plan creates a border across the front of the house, with a striking winter-flowering witch-hazel (*Hamamelis mollis*) planted near the door, giving easy access to its fragrant flowers on late-winter and early-spring days when cold weather might discourage trips farther afield. Colorful wildflowers provide a long season of bloom and cut flowers, and foliage accents give the garden textural interest.

For a nicely layered effect, shrubs and taller perennials are planted closest to the wall, while slightly shorter perennials of varying heights weave together in front. Cheddar pinks (*Dianthus gratianopolitanus*) and thyme form a ruffly edge, lapping over onto the sidewalk, softening its hard edge with their fine-textured foliage. This garden of easy-care plants is designed to work best in a sunny spot that receives at least half a day of sun.

**A fragrant yet robust plant like wormwood, pictured in front at right, is a good choice to edge a walkway, where passersby may brush against its aromatic foliage.**

# A Fragrant Front Yard Garden

# DESIGN AND CULTIVATION TIPS

- The front yard is a highly visible spot, so choose sturdy, reliable plants that will hold up under a range of climatic conditions.

- Expand or contract the design to fit any size lot by planting more or fewer of the shrubs and herbs in the plan. For more dynamic plantings, create odd-numbered groups of three, five, and so on.

- The best way to select scented plants that you'll love is firsthand experience. Spend some time smelling the plants at the nursery before you buy them. This is likely to prolong your shopping beyond one trip—you should see the flowering plants when they are in bloom— but taking that extra time and care will make disappointment less likely.

- Plant early bulbs such as daffodils, hyacinths, and rock garden irises to provide spring bloom and fragrance while you wait for the late-season perennials to fill in. See page 105 for a few suggestions.

## Plants Featured in This Garden

We've only illustrated part of the fragrant front yard garden. For a printer-friendly plan of the entire garden, visit bbg.org/fragrantdesigns.

1  *Agastache aurantiaca* 'Coronado', orange hummingbird mint

2  *Artemisia* 'Powis Castle', wormwood

3  *Asclepias incarnata*, swamp milkweed

4  *Cosmos atrosanguineus*, chocolate cosmos

5  *Dianthus gratianopolitanus*, cheddar pink

6  *Dictamnus albus*, gas plant

7  *Echinacea purpurea* 'Fragrant Angel', purple coneflower

8  *Hamamelis mollis*, Chinese witch-hazel

9  *Rudbeckia subtomentosa*, sweet rudbeckia (not pictured)

10  *Salvia officinalis*, sage

11  *Thymus vulgaris*, garden thyme

12  *Viburnum × juddii*, Judd viburnum

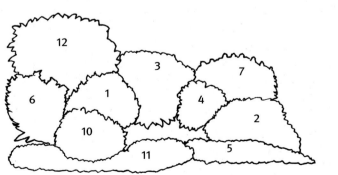

# Plants for a Fragrant Front Yard Garden

*The plants featured in this front yard garden require at least three to four hours of sunshine a day, unless noted otherwise. They will thrive in average garden soil as long as it has good drainage. If your soil tends to be waterlogged, amend it with good-quality compost to improve its structure.*

## *Agastache aurantiaca* 'Coronado' Orange Hummingbird Mint
### Perennial; 2½ feet tall

An upright plant with intensely aromatic, anise-scented foliage, 'Coronado' has beautiful and long-lasting but sadly unscented yellow to orange flowers that are highly attractive to butterflies as well as hummingbirds. Expect a display of blooms from late summer until fall.

**Growing Tips** Bred in North Carolina, 'Coronado' tolerates humidity better than the species, which is a desert native from the Southwest. It can be grown as an annual in colder areas, but it has been frequently reported to survive Zone 4 conditions. Zones 6 to 10.

**Alternatives** 'Apricot Sprite' is a compact cultivar reaching only 18 inches tall; 'Navajo

Sunset' is taller, to 3½ feet. They share the strong anise scent of 'Coronado' and are best grown as annuals in areas with cold and wet winters. *Agastache foeniculum* has blue flowers and strongly licorice-scented leaves. It flowers the first year from seed, so it can also be grown as an annual. Zones 5 to 10.

## *Artemisia* 'Powis Castle' Wormwood
### Woody perennial; 2 to 3 feet tall

This silver-leafed shrub is believed to be a hybrid between the European species *Artemisia absinthum*, the plant flavoring for absinthe, and *A. arborescens*, a favorite Elizabethan strewing herb used to repel fleas. When brushed against, its finely dissected foliage releases a powerful resinous fragrance reminiscent of its parents. Tough and low maintenance, it makes a sparkling silver accent in the border. The summer-blooming yellow flowers are not very ornamental, and some gardeners shear them off.

**Growing Tips** 'Powis Castle' requires a sunny situation but will tolerate a wide range of well-draining soils. In wet situations it can develop rot. Prune it lightly to maintain vigor but never to the ground. Zones 5 to 9.

**Alternatives** Both parents of 'Powis Castle' are grown as ornamentals, and there are many other worthy species of *Artemisia*, such as the beautiful *A. schmidtiana* 'Silver Mound'. *Perovskia atriplicifolia*, Russian sage, page 94, offers another option for a resilient scented silver accent in the garden.

*Cosmos atrosanguineus,* chocolate cosmos

*Asclepias incarnata*, **swamp milkweed**

## *Asclepias incarnata*
## Swamp Milkweed
Perennial; 4 feet tall

An upright and clumping milkweed with narrow leaves on stiff stems that are topped by umbels of strangely architectural pink to white flowers, *Asclepias incarnata* grows and blooms during summer. Its complex flowers have a light, sweet, baby-powder fragrance. This widely distributed North American native is found in marshes and wet meadows. Butterflies love the nectar of swamp milkweed, and it's an important food for the caterpillars of the monarch butterfly.

**Growing Tips** Even though it is usually found on swampy ground in the wild, *Asclepias incarnata* also grows well in ordinary garden soils. It has a long taproot and is difficult to transplant once established, so place with care. The milky sap is slightly toxic. Zones 3 to 7 or 8.

**Alternatives** *Asclepias incarnata* 'Ice Ballet' has white flowers; 'Soulmate' has deep rose flowers and is slightly shorter than the species. *Asclepias speciosa* is a handsome western species with fragrant pink flowers. *Asclepias syriaca,* common milkweed, has stouter foliage and duskier pink flowers but shares the sweet fragrance of the other milkweeds. It is sometimes considered too vigorous for the flower border and may be better suited to a larger wildflower garden. Butterfly weed, *A. tuberosa*, is a beautiful plant and a monarch magnet, but the flowers are not fragrant.

## *Cosmos atrosanguineus*
## Chocolate Cosmos
Perennial; 2½ feet tall

This Mexican native of the aster family has a closer resemblance to a dahlia than to the familiar annual cosmos. Its dark green foliage forms bushy clumps and looks a lot like dahlia foliage, and the tubers can be lifted and stored like dahlias in colder areas. Chocolate cosmos was introduced to horticulture in 1902 and has not been seen in the wild since that time. Because it is self-sterile, it cannot produce seeds, and all plants for sale today are vegetative offspring of the original introduction. The dark red daisylike flowers appear in late summer and are produced in

**Dictamnus albus, gas plant**

abundance until fall. They make good cut flowers and really do smell strongly of chocolate or, to my nose, cocoa powder.

**Growing Tips** Chocolate cosmos needs full sun to perform at its best, so site it in the sunniest corner of your garden. It appreciates heat and thrives in warm weather; winter mulch will increase its hardiness in colder areas. Zones 7 to 9.

**Alternatives** Chocolate flower (*Berlandiera lyrata*), page 90, is a southwestern native ranging from Colorado to Mexico. It is 12 to 36 inches tall with yellow daisylike, chocolate-scented flowers. For large wildflower gardens, *Helianthus grosse-serratus* provides chocolate aroma on a sunflower scale. This native of the Midwest can reach 12 feet tall, has yellow daisy flowers, and blooms in fall.

## *Dianthus gratianopolitanus*
## Cheddar Pink
### Mat-forming perennial; 1 to 12 inches tall

*Dianthus* species have a very long history of cultivation in the garden. The flowers have a strong, distinct clove scent, and in Elizabethan England they were used as a substitute for cloves to flavor wine. The common name for *Dianthus gratianopolitanus* derives from the Cheddar Gorge in England, to which it is native. Cheddar pinks form a dense, low-growing mat of grassy blue to green foliage, which becomes covered with clove-scented pink flowers that persist for weeks in late spring and early summer.

**Growing Tips** Cheddar pinks prefer full sun and slightly alkaline conditions (adding a few chunks of limestone will help sweeten the soil). Deadheading will prolong the bloom period. Because of their small stature and need for good drainage and air circulation, they are best used as an edging at the front of the border. Space plants 6 to 12 inches apart to form a continuous mat. Zones 4 to 8.

**Alternatives** There are many, many garden-worthy species of *Dianthus*, including *D. superbus, caryophyllus,* and *plumarius*, all with the delicious clove-scented flowers. *Dianthus gratianopolitanus* cultivars include 'Firewitch' ('Feuerhexe'), currently a very popular selection. It has deep magenta flowers and tolerates humidity better than other cultivars. 'Tiny Rubies' grows to 4 inches tall and is covered with pink flowers; 'Grandiflorus' grows to 15 inches, with large rose to pink blooms. *Dianthus chinensis* is not fragrant.

## *Dictamnus albus* | Gas Plant
**Perennial; 3 feet tall**

*Dictamnus albus* is a long-lived herbaceous perennial from Europe and central Asia. In nature it is found growing in woodland margins and on rocky screes in lime-rich soils. The lightly anise-scented flowers are showy and can be white, pink, or purple with beautiful dark veins. While these only bloom for a few weeks in late spring or early summer, the flowers are followed by ornamental seed heads. The foliage has a strong lemon scent. The oil in the foliage is reported to ignite in very hot weather, giving *Dictamnus* its common name. It can cause sensitivity in some people, so take care when handling the plant.

**Growing Tips** Rare in the trade because it is slow growing, gas plant is worth hunting for. Low maintenance and tidy, once established it will grow with little care for generations. Because it resents disturbance, place it carefully. Zones 3 to 8.

**Alternatives** *Dictamnus albus* 'Purpureus' has purple flowers. Garden phlox, *Phlox paniculata*, is another old-fashioned, late spring-flowering, scented perennial that persists in the garden for years once established; it sends up beautiful fragrant flower clusters in late spring.

## *Echinacea purpurea* 'Fragrant Angel' | Purple Coneflower
**Perennial; 3 feet tall or more**

The genus *Echinacea* is not normally known for fragrance, but if you get up close, you'll find that many are lightly scented. The white-flowering cultivars of *E. purpurea* seem more fragrant than the purple forms. In the cultivar 'Fragrant Angel', a honeylike fra-

**Echinacea purpurea 'Fragrant Angel', purple coneflower**

grance is combined with the sturdy reliability of native purple coneflower—a hard combination to resist. 'Fragrant Angel' is long blooming, with large (4- to 5-inch) double-ranked rows of white rays around an orange cone. They are produced abundantly from June to August. As with other coneflowers, 'Fragrant Angel' is very attractive to butterflies and, in late fall and winter, the seeds in the cones attract birds. They make long-lasting cut flowers.

**Growing Tips** Though not quite as vigorous as the species, which grows in widely diverse North American habitats, including open woodlands and prairies, *Echinacea purpurea* 'Fragrant Angel' will grow well in full sun to partial shade in ordinary garden soil. Deadheading prolongs flowering, but make sure to leave a few cones on the plant in fall to attract birds. As a bonus, these are great cut flowers. Zones 4 to 9.

**Alternatives** *Echinacea* 'Virgin' is a more compact form of fragrant white coneflower. The pale purple species *E. pallida* also has a light, sweet scent and is a very adaptable garden-worthy perennial.

## Hamamelis mollis
## Chinese Witch-Hazel
**Deciduous shrub; 10 to 15 feet tall**

Witch-hazels are well known for the unusual beauty and fresh fragrance of their long-lasting flowers. They appear on bare branches in late winter and early spring, early enough that the curly twisted petals sometimes get topped with snow. *Hamamelis mollis* is one of the most fragrant of the early-flowering witch-hazels and is more compact than the hybrid *H. × intermedia* and autumn-flowering *H. virginiana* (page 49). On a sunny late-winter day, the sweet yet astringent fragrance carries the distinct promise of spring. A small branch of flowers will fill a room with its clean scent of citrus and spice.

**Growing Tips** Prune Chinese witch-hazel lightly after flowering to remove crossing branches and to control overall shape. Zones 5 to 8.

**Alternatives** *Hamamelis mollis* 'Coombes Wood' has bright yellow flowers. 'Goldcrest' has large golden flowers and blooms later than other cultivars. 'Pallida' has pale lemon flowers; all of these cultivars are fragrant.

## Rudbeckia subtomentosa
## Sweet Rudbeckia
**Prairie perennial; 3 to 5 feet tall**

Sweet rudbeckia, native to the central U.S. prairies, is an easy, low-maintenance plant for the back of the border. The tall, bushy green foliage is anise-scented and topped by masses of bloom. The bright yellow flowers are 3 inches wide with dark centers and are produced over a long period from late summer to fall. They have a mild licorice scent that is very attractive to butterflies.

**Growing Tips** Sweet rudbeckia is an easygoing plant that thrives in full sun and tolerates heat and humidity to boot. Taller plants may need support. Zones 4 to 9.

**Alternatives** *Rudbeckia subtomentosa* 'Henry Eilers' has sweetly vanilla-scented foliage and unusual quilled rays that give the flowers a striking starburst appearance.

## Salvia officinalis | Sage
**Evergreen shrub; 2½ feet tall**

This spreading shrub from the dry, rocky Mediterranean basin has gray-green foliage with a strong woodsy-camphor scent. It produces pretty but unscented purple or blue flowers in late spring and is very attractive to bees and butterflies. Sage has been used as a culinary and medicinal herb in Europe since ancient times, and its essential oil has antiseptic and antifungal properties.

**Growing Tips** Sage grows best in full sun in well-drained soil. Older plants may become woody and need replacement. Harvesting sage leaves by light pruning can help keep the plants compact. Zones 4 to 8.

**Alternatives** There are many good cultivars of *Salvia officinalis*, some of which have colorful foliage, including the gold-variegated 'Aurea'; purple-leafed 'Purpurescens'; and the unusual 'Tricolor', which has green-and-white leaves tinged with purple.

*Rudbeckia subtomentosa*, **sweet rudbeckia**

*Viburnum × juddii*, Judd viburnum

## *Thymus vulgaris* | Garden Thyme
Shrub; 6 to 12 inches tall

Native to the arid Mediterranean region, low-growing garden thyme is evergreen in mild climates. Thyme has small, cupped, gray-green leaves that smell pungent and sweet with tannin and citrus notes. The pale purple flowers are not considered very ornamental, but the blooms are sought after by bees and butterflies.

**Growing Tips** Garden thyme demands super drainage and full sun but is not otherwise particular. Once established it can be quite drought tolerant. Plants become bare-stemmed and woody over time and so should occasionally be replaced or propagated by cuttings. Light shearing to harvest the leaves help the plant remain bushy. Zones 5 to 9.

**Alternatives** *Thymus vulgaris* 'Argenteus' has very attractive silver foliage. Lemon thyme (*T. × citriodorus*) is a hybrid between *T. vulgaris* and *T. pulegioides* with a strong lemon scent. Cultivars include spring-green 'Lime', and 'Silver Queen', which has leaves edged in white.

## *Viburnum × juddii*
## Judd Viburnum
Deciduous shrub; 8 feet tall

The handsome *Viburnum × juddii* combines the strong, sweet clove flower scent of its parent *V. carlesii* with a denser habit and larger blossoms. Pink buds emerge in April along with the foliage and expand into large, white flowers that can fill a garden with their delicious sweet-spicy fragrance. The leaves are a nice dark green and turn to burgundy-red in the autumn.

**Growing Tips** Judd viburnum is a slow-growing, trouble-free shrub that is not particular about soil and is drought tolerant once established. It will produce more flowers and turn a nicer red in fall when given more sun. Prune only immediately after flowering to preserve next year's bloom. Zones 4 to 8.

**Alternatives** There are many good garden viburnums, though not all have scented blooms. The best fragrant selections include *Viburnum × burkwoodii*, *V. carlesii*, and *V. × carlcephalum*, which all share a spicy fragrance and have many cultivars available.

# Wildlife-Friendly Fragrant Hell Strips

Claire Hagen Dole

Commonly defined as the narrow strip of land between sidewalk and street, city-owned but maintained by the homeowner, the curbside hell strip presents special challenges for landscaping. Hot and dry, assaulted by salt, sand, and passing dogs, this harsh environment requires first-class survivors, able to handle whatever weather and urban life can dish out. Look to Mediterranean herbs, such as lavender and rosemary, for their intoxicating fragrance, interesting form, and foliage that invites touching. Southwestern natives, including many *Salvia* and *Agastache* species, are equally at home in dry, nutrient-poor soils and provide a variety of shapes, scents, and textures. Midwestern prairie wildflowers and grasses are another source of abuse-tolerant plants, with breathtaking beauty and diversity.

The hell strip presented here has been designed to provide scent and color over many months, from the bright yellow flowers of lemon daylily in spring to the airy sprays of bluebeard in late fall. A color palette of pinks, purples, and blues is accented in late summer by the hot orange blossoms of marigold and sunset hyssop. Later, the foliage of prairie dropseed becomes golden, forming a beautiful backdrop to sage's deep blue flowers.

The garden gains interest from variations in texture: Leaves are grasslike or ferny, wide or narrow; flowers range from dainty (alyssum) to fuzzy (coyote mint) to bell-shaped (daylily). The range of plant sizes from ground-hugging to chest-high also helps to keep things lively. Shrubs and ornamental grasses provide structure during winter and look good powdered with snow. A wonderful bonus of this fragrant hell strip is its great attractiveness to wildlife—watch the garden come to life in spring with the busy hum of bees and bumblebees and the motion of butterflies and hummingbirds seeking nectar. In fall, songbirds are drawn to the nutritious seed heads and to the ground below, where prairie dropseed has released its small, round seeds.

Unless you live in a community with strict landscaping covenants, the usually dull piece of curb acreage can easily be transformed into a vibrant neighborhood attraction. Before breaking ground, talk to your neighbors about your plans for creating a fragrant, wildlife- and people-friendly curbside garden. Your enthusiasm might spark a local gardening trend.

**It might look fragile, but English lavender is a resilient plant with sturdy flowers that's up to the rough-and-tumble of a low-maintenance garden planted between sidewalk and curb.**

# A Wildlife-Friendly Fragrant Hell Strip

# DESIGN AND CULTIVATION TIPS

- Consult local ordinances and neighborhood covenants about plant heights and landscaping styles before you start digging to make sure whatever you plant meets requirements. If the hell strip is beneath utility lines, consider the mature height of your plants. Call a utilities locator service for information on buried wires and cables. You may also need to obtain your municipal authority's permission if you plan to plant trees and may have to choose from a list of approved species.

- Leave a foot-wide strip next to the curb clear to enable people to easily get in and out of parked cars. Plant it with a tough groundcover, such as wild strawberry, or place pavers along the curb's edge.

- Create walkways from sidewalk to curb, so visitors can meander between plants, stopping to touch and sniff leaves and blossoms. Plant some creeping thyme to soften the edges of pavers and give off a scent when stepped on. Install a birdbath nearby for a supply of fresh water. Add a touch of surprise with a small boulder, up to 3 feet wide and 1 foot high, or choose a few quirky pieces of art.

- Focus on drought-tolerant plants suitable for your region to minimize the need for supplemental watering. Choose compact cultivars of taller species to make it easier to comply with local regulations. Water plants during the first season to allow them to establish strong root systems. In following years, water during extreme drought. If a plant doesn't thrive, replace it.

- Plan for a seasonal display of bloom and fragrance, from early spring into autumn. Plant bulbs of fragrant *Crocus crysanthus* to peek up through groundcover in early spring. Deadhead fall flowers to prolong bloom until frost.

## Plants Featured in This Garden

For a printer-friendly garden plan drawn to scale, visit bbg.org/fragrantdesigns.

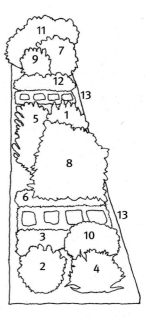

1  *Agastache rupestris,* sunset hyssop
2  *Caryopteris × clandonensis* 'Petit Bleu', bluebeard
3  *Dianthus gratianopolitanus* 'Tiny Rubies', cheddar pink
4  *Hemerocallis lilioasphodelus,* lemon daylily
5  *Lavandula angustifolia* 'Hidcote', English lavender
6  *Lobularia maritima* 'Royal Carpet', alyssum
7  *Monardella villosa,* coyote mint
8  *Rosa virginiana,* Virginia rose
9  *Salvia farinacea* 'Victoria Blue', mealycup sage
10 *Santolina chamaecyparissus* 'Nana', lavender cotton
11 *Sporobolus heterolepis,* prairie dropseed
12 *Tagetes tenuifolia* 'Tangerine Gem', signet marigold
13 *Thymus serpyllum,* creeping thyme

# Plants for a Wildlife-Friendly Fragrant Hell Strip

*Most plants in this garden require at least six hours of sun and well-drained soil. Once established, the shrubs and perennials are drought tolerant, but keep them well watered in their first season to foster strong root systems.*

## Agastache rupestris
### Sunset Hyssop
**Perennial; 2 feet tall**

A member of the mint family, *Agastache rupestris* hails from the Southwest and has small tubular flowers in shades of orange and reddish purple that attract hummingbirds. The narrow, gray-green leaves emit a pungent, spicy scent like licorice when rubbed. The plant's soft, delicate appearance belies its toughness. It blooms from midsummer to frost and makes a great cut flower.

**Growing Tips** Cut off spent flower spikes to keep it blooming well into fall. In cold climates, sunset hyssop may be coaxed into overwintering by mulching with gravel; Propagate by seed or take cuttings in summer. Zones 5 to 9.

**Alternatives** Long-blooming *Agastache* 'Blue Fortune' attracts butterflies to its 3- to 4-foot powder-blue flower spikes. The toothed leaves have a strong anise scent, as do those of Texas hummingbird mint (*A. cana*), which is covered with dark pink flowers through fall and grows to 3 feet.

## Caryopteris × clandonensis
### 'Petit Bleu' | Bluebeard
**Shrub; 2 to 3 feet tall**

'Petit Bleu' is a compact, bushy cross between two species of *Caryopteris* that are native to dry, rocky regions with poor soils in China, Japan, Korea, and Mongolia. From late summer through fall, its tight flower clusters form an airy cloud of deep blue that attract late-season butterflies. Though the flowers are not scented, the glossy, dark green leaves give off a minty scent when rubbed.

**Growing Tips** In colder climates (Zones 5 and below), the foliage of bluebeard dies back to the ground. Prune it hard in early spring to encourage new growth. Zones 5 to 9.

**Alternatives** *Caryopteris* × *clandoensis* 'First Choice' is a compact shrub with dark purplish-blue flowers. 'Longwood Blue' reaches 4 feet high and has violet-blue flowers and silvery leaves. 'Summer Sorbet' has variegated, yellow-edged leaves and pale blue flowers. It is 3 feet tall. All three have mint-scented foliage and no floral scent.

## Dianthus gratianopolitanus
### 'Tiny Rubies' | Cheddar Pink
**Short-lived perennial; 4 inches tall**

See page 28.

*Caryopteris* × *clandonensis*, **bluebeard**

***Hemerocallis lilioasphodelus,*** **lemon daylily**

## *Hemerocallis lilioasphodelus*
## Lemon Daylily

**Perennial; 1 to 3 feet tall and wide**

Among the hundreds of *Hemerocallis* cultivars available, lemon daylily has endured as a popular species plant. Smaller and daintier than the bicolor cultivars, its yellow flowers also send out a delicious citrus scent. Lemon daylily blooms all summer long, each flower lasting for only one day. A favorite in English cottage gardens, it was brought to the New World by early settlers. Of somewhat obscure origin (possibly China), lemon daylily is now naturalized in Europe in rocky mountain woods, wet meadows, and riversides on foothills of the Alps.

**Growing Tips** Daylilies do well in many climate and soil conditions, but they need good drainage. Plant tubers 1 inch deep and 18 to 20 inches apart in compost-enriched soil. Remove spent flowers to prolong blooming. In fall, remove seedpods and dead foliage. Lemon daylily thrives for years without attention, but you can divide clumps to make more plants. Zones 3 to 9.

**Alternatives** *Hemerocallis* 'Stella de Oro' is a popular cultivar that grows to 1 foot high. Its trumpet-shaped flowers are yellow with a golden throat and have a light, sweet fragrance. Plant groups of 'Stella de Oro' to make a tidy groundcover.

## *Lavandula angustifolia* 'Hidcote'
## English or Common Lavender

**Perennial; 1 to 1½ feet tall**

Rich in essential oils, the species *Lavandula angustifolia* is grown commercially for the classic "true lavender" scent. The essential oil is distilled from glands in tiny hairs on the flowers, leaves, and stems. Lavender flowers have a scent similar to the leaves but not as strong; these are sometimes used in cooking. The cultivar 'Hidcote', a dwarf version of this Mediterranean native, forms upright clumps up to 1½ feet in height. Dark purple flowers rise on stalks above the foliage all summer long and attract bees and butterflies. The narrow, gray-green foliage is also aromatic. In mild climates, 'Hidcote' stays evergreen in winter, providing nice color and structure to the garden.

*Santolina chamaecyparissus* 'Nana', lavender cotton

**Growing Tips** Space plants 2 feet apart to allow good air circulation. Cut back by a third in spring to shape and encourage new growth; then deadhead after flowering. In cold climates, site lavender in a sunny, sheltered spot and mulch during the winter. 'Hidcote' makes a nice low hedge or edging plant. Zones 5 to 8.

**Alternatives** *Lavandula angustifolia* 'Nana' forms a dense mound of blue-gray leaves and blue flowers. Growing only about 10 inches high, it looks good in a rock garden as well as near the front of a border. It is hardy in Zones 5 to 10. Spanish lavender (*L. stoechas*), hardy in Zones 7 to 10, has showy purple flower heads with upright bracts. It grows 2 to 3 feet high and has a strong, resiny fragrance.

## *Lobularia maritima*
### 'Royal Carpet' | Alyssum
Tender perennial, often grown as annual; 4 to 8 inches tall

See page 81.

## *Monardella villosa*
### Coyote Mint
Tender perennial; 2 feet tall and wide

Native to California's coastal range, coyote mint is a sprawling plant with dark green, fuzzy leaves that give off a strong, minty scent when brushed. Native Americans have used it to make a tea. From spring through summer, it is covered with round clusters of purple blossoms, the nectar of which is highly attractive to butterflies and hummingbirds.

**Growing Tips** Coyote mint grows best in full sun to light shade. Deadhead spent flowers to encourage more blooms. In mild climates, prune heavily in late winter. It is not winter hardy in cold climates; take cuttings in fall to overwinter in a cold frame or start seeds indoors in spring. Zones 8 to 10.

**Alternatives** The approximately 20 species of *Monardella* are valued as native western wildflowers. The genus is closely related to *Monarda*, which has many garden species and cultivars. Bergamot (*M. fistulosa*) is a tall prairie plant with a strong minty scent and lightly fragrant purple flowers that bloom in midsummer. Held upright on stiff stems, the flowers attract many different butterflies.

## Rosa virginiana
## Virginia Rose
**Shrub; to 6 feet tall and wide**

Native to northeastern North America, Virginia rose forms clusters of single, pink flowers with a sweet, "old-rose" fragrance from early summer to midsummer. Its glossy, dark green leaves turn crimson in autumn, complementing the large red rosehips and reddish, hooked prickles. Virginia rose is very attractive to bees and bumblebees. In winter, birds feed on its fruit.

**Growing Tips** Cold hardy, disease resistant, and salt tolerant, Virginia rose grows in a wide range of soil conditions. Choose a sunny location with good drainage. Prune lightly in late winter to shape it, and as it spreads by suckering, remove shoots at the base to keep it in check. Zones 3 to 8.

**Alternatives** Carolina rose (*Rosa carolina*) is an East Coast native with single, pink blossoms that appear in early summer. It reaches 3 feet high and may spread to form thickets. Plant in full sun and water regularly during drought. Its fall color is not showy, but the red hips attract birds. Zones 4 to 9.

## Salvia farinacea 'Victoria Blue'
## Mealycup Sage
**Tender perennial, often grown as annual; 1 to 2 feet tall and wide**

This dwarf cultivar of southwestern prairies and plains native *Salvia farinacea* has sage-scented, grayish-green leaves, topped by spikes of blue-purple grape-scented blooms. The stalk and blossoms are fuzzy or "mealy," hence its common name. The flower spikes over the foliage attract butterflies, bees, and hummingbirds from summer through fall.

**Growing Tips** Deadhead 'Victoria Blue' or prune it back to encourage regrowth in late

summer. In humid climates, avoid powdery mildew by spacing 12 to 15 inches apart for air circulation. Zones 8 to 10.

**Alternatives** Blue anise sage, *Salvia guaranitica* 'Black and Blue,' has oval, pointed leaves with an anise-and-sage scent and hummingbird-luring deep blue flowers. It reaches 3 to 4 feet high and blooms from midsummer to frost. Prune hard in late winter to shape the plant and control its size. Grow as an annual in cold climates. Zones 7 to 10.

## Santolina chamaecyparissus
## 'Nana' | Lavender Cotton
**Perennial; 1 foot tall**

*Santolina*, native to the dry, rocky hills around the Mediterranean, has dense, silvery aromatic foliage that made it essential in Elizabethan knot gardens, where it was used as hedging surrounding other herbs. 'Nana' is a dwarf cultivar that reaches 1 foot in height and forms a soft mound. Finely cut leaves on woolly white stems give off a pungent, resinous scent. In summer, button-shaped yellow flowers cover the plant.

*Salvia farinacea* 'Victoria Blue', mealycup sage

**Growing Tips** 'Nana' is tolerant of salt spray but does not like humidity. Cut back in early spring to shape new growth. If you wish to accent the foliage, flowers can be sheared off. It is evergreen in mild climates but needs to be mulched in colder areas, where it will die back before sending out new growth in spring. Zones 6 to 9.

**Alternatives** The species grows to 2 feet, with silvery gray-green leaves that are less aromatic than those of 'Nana.' *Santolina chamaecyparissus* 'Lemon Queen' has pale yellow flowers against finely cut, silvery sweet-scented foliage.

## *Sporobolus heterolepis*
## Prairie Dropseed
**Perennial grass; to 2 feet tall and wide, with flower spikes to 4 feet tall**

Midwest native prairie dropseed forms gracefully arching clumps of fine-textured leaves, which turn from green to golden orange in autumn. In late summer, small flowers form on long stems, giving off a scent described as buttered popcorn and cilantro. Dropseed gets its name from the small, round seeds that fall to the ground in fall. These nutritious seeds

were gathered and made into flour by Native Americans and are eagerly sought out by birds. Prairie dropseed makes a nice curbside border or meadow planting interspersed with prairie flowers.

**Growing Tips** *Sporobolus heterolepis* is slow to establish from seed, so plant nursery-grown clumps if you want a mature-looking planting in less than three to five years. If you buy specimens in 3-inch pots and plant them in spring, you'll get flowers in the first season, but the plants will be small for the first couple of years as they build their root systems. To have mature-sized plants by the second season, buy them in gallon pots from a reputable nursery and space the plants 18 to 24 inches apart. Cut back the dried grass once in late winter. Prairie dropseed rarely self-seeds; divide clumps in spring or fall to increase plants. Zones 3 to 9.

**Alternatives** Alkali dropseed (*Sporobolus airoides*) is a lovely but unscented southwestern native that grows to 3 feet tall and wide. It forms airy clusters of delicate pink flowers, and the foliage turns yellow in fall. For a scented alternative, lemon grass (*Cymbopogon citratus*), page 70, is a subtropical clumping grass with lemon-scented, yellow-green foliage. It reaches 3 to 4 feet tall and wide and tolerates dry soil but needs additional water in drought. Treat it as an annual in cold climates. Zones 9 to 10.

## *Tagetes tenuifolia* 'Tangerine Gem' | Signet Marigold
**Annual; 1 to 2 feet tall and wide**

Signet marigolds form dainty mounds of ferny, lemon-scented foliage topped by many small, single-petaled flowers. The bright orange petals of 'Tangerine Gem' are edible and add a colorful, tangy note to salads. Native to Mexico, this drought-tolerant annual blooms from midsummer until frost. It attracts small butterflies, such as blues and hairstreaks.

*Tagetes tenuifolia* 'Tangerine Gem', signet marigold

**_Sporobolus heterolepis_, prairie dropseed**

**Growing Tips** Marigolds are easy to grow from seed in average soil and full sun to partial shade. Mulch to conserve moisture, and water during drought. Remove spent flowers to encourage more blooming. Signet marigolds look great in containers or as a border to a walkway or flower bed.

**Alternatives** _Tagetes tenuifolia_ 'Lemon Gem' and 'Paprika Gem' offer yellow or red alternatives with the same delicate, lemon-scented foliage and single-petaled flowers. French marigold (_T. patula_, page 84) has single or double petals.

## _Thymus serpyllum_
### Creeping Thyme
#### Perennial groundcover; 2 to 3 inches tall

Creeping thyme forms a spreading, low-growing mat with tiny gray-green leaves that release a sweet, herbal scent when brushed or stepped upon. From early summer through fall, it is covered with deep pink/purple flowers that attract bees. A Mediterranean native in the mint family, it has long been a favorite for softening the edges of paving stones or rock walls.

**Growing Tips** Creeping thyme withstands moderate foot traffic. Once established, it needs little care. Avoid planting it in damp spots, where it will rot. Propagate by division or by cutting rooted stems. Evergreen in mild winters. Zones 4 to 10.

**Alternatives** _Thymus serpyllum_ 'Albus' forms white flowers in early summer; it is fast-spreading and reaches 2 to 6 inches tall. The culitivar 'Goldstream' forms a tight mat of lemon-scented variegated leaves and pink flowers and grows 1 to 2 inches tall. _Thymus praecox_ 'Coconut' is a low-growing, spreading thyme with pink flowers and coconut-scented leaves.

# Fragrant Native Woodland Gardens

Janet Marinelli

For aficionados of the wild woodlands of southeastern Canada and the eastern United States, nothing is more captivating than a garden filled with fragrant denizens of the native forests. By bringing together groups of different-sized plants you can easily create a naturalistic, layered garden that will quickly become a rich habitat for a wide range of wildlife.

The backyard-scale garden featured here includes all the overlapping vertical layers of a natural woodland, with one large canopy tree, a smaller understory tree, a few large shrubs, some smaller shrubs, wildflowers, and a groundcover with handsome glossy and aromatic foliage. Carolina jessamine (*Gelsemium sempervirens*), a fragrant vine, clambers over a rustic arbor leading to a woodland path that meanders through the garden. The path ends at an Adirondack-style swinging loveseat that invites you to linger and enjoy the fragrance and flowers from earliest spring, when spicebush blooms add a soft yellow flush to woodlands awakening from winter, until the end of autumn, when the pungent scent of witch-hazel flowers fills the air. The garden is a cool, shady refuge from summer's sun and heat.

Most of the plants in this fragrant woodland garden have scented flowers, and a few, including wintergreen, witch-hazel, and spicebush, have aromatic leaves or bark. Some of the species, like large fothergilla (*Fothergilla major*), are naturally rare, and others, such as Carolina allspice (*Calycanthus floridus*) and woodland phlox (*Phlox divaricata*), have disappeared from the wild in some states and are declining in others. By planting them, you can help ensure the survival of these lovely plants.

None of the plants in this garden of fragrant natives is difficult to grow. Although they're not fussy, they thrive in the partial shade and moist soils rich in organic matter that are found in the woodlands they inhabit.

This garden is suitable for a wide swath of forested eastern North America, from southeastern Canada to the southeastern U.S., west to Ontario, the Dakotas, and Texas. If you live in California, the Pacific Northwest, or the deserts of the Southwest, or if you are a prairie gardener, you'll find a chart of appropriate native regional alternatives online at bbg.org/fragrantdesigns.

**Unlike Chinese witch-hazels, which bloom in early spring, American witch-hazel's spicily fragrant flowers light up the garden in late fall.**

# A Small Fragrant Native Woodland Garden

# DESIGN AND CULTIVATION TIPS

- If your garden is small, eliminate the large canopy tree (Kentucky coffee tree), and grow the shrubs and wildflowers beneath a smaller flowering tree such as white fringe tree or sweetbay magnolia.

- The "secret ingredient" for a successful native woodland garden is mulch, which helps moderate soil temperatures, conserves moisture, and enriches the soil as it breaks down over time. Reapply mulch annually in autumn. When the leaves fall, shred them or run your lawnmower over them a few times, then apply them to your planting beds.

- Plan to spend time in your garden observing the pollinators and other wildlife that have evolved with these native plants over the eons, from the wild silk moths that frequent the Kentucky coffee tree to the beautiful spicebush swallowtails that lay their eggs on the shrub for which they are named.

## Plants Featured in This Garden

For a printer-friendly garden plan drawn to scale, visit bbg.org/fragrantdesigns.

1   *Calycanthus floridus*, Carolina allspice
2   *Chionanthus virginicus*, white fringe tree
3   *Clethra alnifolia*, summersweet, sweet pepperbush
4   *Fothergilla major*, large fothergilla
5   *Gaultheria procumbens*, wintergreen, teaberry
6   *Gelsemium sempervirens*, Carolina jessamine
7   *Gymnocladus dioica*, Kentucky coffee tree
8   *Hamamelis virginiana*, American witch-hazel
9   *Lindera benzoin*, spicebush
10  *Phlox divaricata*, woodland phlox, wild sweet William
11  *Rhododendron prinophyllum* (syn. *R. roseum*), rose-shell azalea
12  *Viola blanda*, sweet white violet

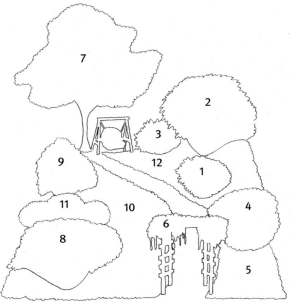

# Plants for a Fragrant Native Woodland Garden

*Most plants featured in this garden will thrive with a few hours of sunshine in average moist garden soil that is slightly acidic, but they are usually very adaptable to a wide variety of light, soil, and moisture conditions.*

## Calycanthus floridus
## Carolina Allspice
Shrub; 6 to 10 feet tall and wide

This shrub's leathery leaves, which are dark green above and grayish green below, turn soft yellow in fall, exposing misshapen seed-pods when they fall. The dark reddish-brown flowers, 2 inches across, have a fruity fragrance and are pollinated by beetles. They bloom in late spring to summer, continuing sporadically until fall. When bruised, the stems are also aromatic. Carolina allspice is found in and along the edges of deciduous woodlands, along stream banks, and on moist hillsides from Maryland to Missouri and south from Florida to Louisiana.

**Growing Tips** Carolina allspice adapts to many soil types but does best with some sun and moist soil. Zones 4 to 9.

**Alternatives** Virginia sweetspire, *Itea virginica*, bears tassels of fragrant, starry white flowers that are butterfly magnets in spring.

## Chionanthus virginicus
## White Fringe Tree
Small tree; 12 to 20 feet tall and wide

White fringe tree's primary attraction is its sweetly scented flowers—drooping, 8-inch-long clusters of airy, fringelike, creamy-white petals—which open before or with the first leaves in April to May. Female flowers give way to clusters of dark bluish-black, olivelike fruits in late summer that are eaten by wildlife. For a good crop of fruit, plant a male and female near each other. The glossy, dark green, spear-shaped leaves turn yellow in autumn. White fringe tree, native to rich, moist woods from New Jersey to Missouri and south from Florida to Texas, is the host plant for caterpillars of the rustic sphinx moth.

**Growing Tips** White fringe tree does best in partial shade and rich, moist, well-drained soil. Tolerant of air pollution, it adapts well to urban settings. Zones 3 to 9.

**Alternatives** Sweetbay magnolia, *Magnolia virginiana*, is a lovely tree suitable for small gardens, with creamy-white, 2- to 3-inch-wide, heavenly sweet-scented blooms.

## Clethra alnifolia | Summersweet
Shrub; 5 to 8 feet tall and 4 to 6 feet wide

Summersweet is one of the best mid- to late-summer bloomers. Its oval, glossy, dark green leaves turn yellow in autumn. Wonderfully sweet and slightly spicy, its upright, 3- to 5-inch-long flower spikes, typically creamy

*Calycanthus floridus*, Carolina allspice

*Fothergilla major*, large fothergilla

white but sometimes pink, are as lovely to smell as they are to look at and perfume the sultry summer air for weeks. The flowers last four to six weeks in July and August and attract bees and other pollinators. Its native habitat is moist woods and swamps in eastern states from Massachusetts to Texas.

**Growing Tips** Summersweet thrives in moist but well-drained soil in full sun to dappled shade but is very adaptable to other conditions except hot, dry sites. Zones 4 to 9.

**Alternatives** To my mind, there's no alternative to summersweet. However, there are a number of cultivars. Among the most popular are 'Hummingbird', growing to 3 feet tall and wide; 'Ruby Spice', with the darkest pink blooms; and 'Sixteen Candles', a compact selection with upright spires of white flowers.

## *Fothergilla major*
### Large Fothergilla
Shrub; 6 feet tall

This densely branched plant has picturesque crooked stems and dark blue-green leaves that become spectacular in fall, coloring red, orange, and yellow. The 1- to 3-inch-long

white bottlebrush flower spikes emit a rich honey fragrance in April to May. The flowers, which appear before the leaves emerge, have showy yellow stamens with long filaments. It is native to rich upland woods in the southern Appalachians and adjacent Piedmont plateau.

**Growing Tips** Large fothergilla prefers moist to dry well-drained, slightly acidic soil. Even though the shrub is very shade tolerant, it will bloom best in a spot where in receives two or three hours of sun. It is extremely insect and disease resistant. Zones 4 to 8.

**Alternatives** Dwarf fothergilla, *F. gardenii*, is smaller than large fothergilla, as its common name suggests, and generally has smaller and earlier-blooming flowers.

## *Gaultheria procumbens*
### Wintergreen, Teaberry
Evergreen groundcover; 4 to 8 inches tall

Wintergreen is a groundcover with year-round appeal. It forms a dense low carpet of shiny leaves, which take on a deep burgundy tinge in winter. From May through summer,

*Gaultheria procumbens*, **wintergreen or teaberry**

petite urn-shaped, nodding white flowers touched with pale pink appear at the base of the leaves. The flowers develop into showy, ½-inch, bright scarlet fruits in summer. Wintergreen foliage is wonderfully aromatic when crushed. Still used in wintergreen tea, the leaves are also distilled to make an essential oil. Wintergreen is native to pine and hardwood forests from Newfoundland and New England west to Minnesota, south to Georgia in the mountains.

**Growing Tips** Wintergreen mainly occurs on moist sites but tolerates moisture conditions ranging from dry to poorly drained. It likes an acidic, moist, organic soil and light shade in the north and medium to heavy shade farther south. Zones 3 to cooler parts of 8.

**Alternatives** *Pycnanthemum muticum*, mountain mint, has aromatic minty leaves like wintergreen but grows taller, to 3 feet, and likes at least partial sun. Mountain mint produces dense clusters of tiny pinkish flowers, highlighted by silvery bracts, that draw a wide variety of butterflies, especially smaller ones.

## *Gelsemium sempervirens*
## Carolina Jessamine

### Perennial vine; 15 feet tall or more

Carolina jessamine is a beautiful and restrained vine. Its lustrous, dark green leaves, which are evergreen in the South, set off the yellow flowers beautifully. The foliage turns slightly yellow or purplish in winter. Its yellow, trumpet-shaped flowers have a lightly sweet fragrance and are a sure sign of spring in its native environs, woodland clearings and open fields from Virginia to Arkansas, and south from Florida to Texas.

**Growing Tips** Carolina jessamine prefers evenly moist, fertile soils but is a very adaptable plant that can tolerate some drought and heavy clay or sandy soils. It also tolerates considerable shade, but for profuse blooming it needs three to four hours of sun a day. Because it is a twining vine, it looks best climbing on a fence, trellis, or other support, or spilling over a wall. Zones 6 to 9.

**Alternatives** In the north, plant hardier selections such as the cultivar 'Margarita', which is reliably hardy in Zone 6.

*Wisteria frutescens*, American wisteria (page 110), produces chains of gorgeous purple or white flowers.

## Gymnocladus dioica
### Kentucky Coffee Tree
Tree; 60 to 75 feet tall and
30 to 50 feet wide

Kentucky coffee tree is an uncommon tree with an open canopy of large, twice-compound leaves that turn yellow in fall. In May to June, female trees produce large, 8- to 12-inch-long inflorescences with tiny greenish-white flowers (male inflorescences are about a third as long as females'). The flowers aren't showy, but they have a lovely roselike fragrance. Bees find them hard to resist. The female flowers mature into large, leathery, 5- to 10-inch seedpods resembling giant peapods. These turn brown and remain on the tree through winter. The tree is a host plant for the caterpillars of wild silk moths. It is native to woods, floodplains, old fields, and clearings from Maine to Ontario and North Dakota, and south from Atlanta to Texas.

**Growing Tips** Kentucky coffee tree grows in a wide range of soil types, though it prefers rich soils, and needs at least six hours of midday sun to do well. It is resistant to disease and insect problems and tolerant of city conditions. Zones 3 to 8.

**Alternatives** American linden (*Tilia americana*) is a lure for bees. Southern magnolia (*Magnolia grandiflora*) has creamy-white blossoms that may be a foot in diameter and have a fragrance "better than the best perfume," in the words of woody plant maven Michael Dirr. Zones 7 to 9.

## Hamamelis virginiana
### American Witch-Hazel
Shrub; 12 feet tall

When most plants have dropped their leaves and gone to seed, American witch-hazel provides a dazzling late-fall display of flowers that appear October to December, usually on bare branches but sometimes together with the apricot-yellow autumn foliage. American witch-hazel is not as fragrant as Chinese witch-hazel (page 30) or popular hybrids, but those all bloom in early spring. American witch-hazel is a multitrunked shrub with an attractive vase-shaped habit. Its pungently scented, spidery flowers each have four crinkly, streamerlike petals that are yellow and sometimes tinged with orange or red. The bark traditionally has been steeped in water to produce a mild, spicy astringent. American witch-hazel's native habitat is woodlands, forest margins, and stream banks from the maritime provinces to Ontario and south from Florida to Texas.

**Growing Tips** American witch-hazel performs best in moist, slightly acidic soils rich in organic matter, in partial sun to light shade, but it tolerates a range of conditions except extremely dry locations. Once established, witch-hazel requires little care other than a heavy pruning in early spring once every decade or so to maintain its attractive shape. Zones 3 to 8.

**Gymnocladus dioica, Kentucky coffee tree**

**Alternatives** Spring witch-hazel (*Hamamelis vernalis*), native to the Ozarks, has smaller flowers than *H. virginiana* and is also fragrant, with a hint of jasmine. Instead of autumn, the blooms appear in late winter, even in the snow. Zones 4 to 8.

## *Lindera benzoin* | Spicebush
### Shrub; 6 to 15 feet tall

Other than skunk cabbage, marsh marigold, and spring witch-hazel, spicebush is the only thing going for woodland insects in early spring, when its small yellow flowers bloom on still-leafless branches, adding a soft yellow flush to forests just beginning to awaken from winter. In summer, flowers on the female plants develop into oily, oval-shaped fruits that ripen to bright scarlet and are quite eye-catching against the brilliant yellow fall foliage, if you can find them before the birds. Along with sassafras, it's the preferred host for the caterpillars of the spicebush swallowtail butterfly. Although the shrub's delicate little yellow flowers are sweetly fragrant, it is the scent of its leaves and bark—a mixture of cloves, anise, and musk—that give it its name. The native habitat of spicebush is moist woods and swamps from Maine to Ontario and Michigan and south from Florida to Texas.

**Growing Tips** These are not fussy plants, but moist, fertile soil and partial shade are ideal. Zones 4 to 9.

**Alternatives** Pondberry or southern spicebush (*Lindera melissifolia*) is a rare native of the southeastern states with leaves that have a strong lemon-sassafras fragrance when crushed. Zones 8 to 11. The leaves of bog spicebush (*L. subcoriacea*), also rare and found in the Southeast, are faintly aromatic when young but become odorless with age. Zones 7 to 9.

## *Phlox divaricata* | Woodland Phlox, Wild Sweet William
### Perennial wildflower; 1 foot tall

There are numerous native phlox species, but to me, none are as elegant or fragrant as woodland phlox. It bears loose, flat clusters of delicate, spice-scented flowers in spring in just about every shade of blue, forming a fragrant carpet that lasts for a month. Butterflies and moths love the flowers. This phlox self-sows, slowly forming natural drifts, which are especially lovely when planted as a ground-cover with native spring-blooming azaleas. It is native to moist, rich deciduous woods in Quebec and Ontario, and from Vermont to South Dakota, south from Florida to Texas.

**Growing Tips** Woodland phlox prefers partial to full shade and moist soils rich in organic matter. Once it's finished flowering, woodland phlox isn't exactly a looker, so interplant it with some ferns, Solomon's seal (*Polygonatum biflorum*), and other wildflowers with bolder foliage. Zones 3 to 8.

**Alternatives** A few woodland phlox cultivars are extra fragrant, especially *Phlox divaricata* 'Clouds of Perfume', with icy-blue flowers, and 'Blue Perfume', with purple-blue blooms.

*Lindera benzoin*, **spicebush**

*Phlox divaricata*, **woodland phlox or wild sweet William**

## *Rhododendron prinophyllum* (syn. *R. roseum*) | Rose-Shell Azalea
Shrub; 4 to 8 feet tall and wide

The most fragrant of the spring-blooming azaleas, rose-shell azalea has large clusters of bright pink, funnel-shaped flowers with a penetrating clove scent that carries far and wide. Its numerous spreading branches are covered with smooth blue-green foliage that turns bronzy or purplish in fall. It is native to damp thickets and open woods in eastern North America west to Illinois and south from North Carolina to Texas.

**Growing Tips** Partial shade and organically rich, moisture-retentive but well-drained soils are key to growing this species. Its shallow, fibrous root system should never be allowed to dry out, so mulching with bark or pine needles is recommended to retain moisture and stabilize soil temperature. Zones 3 to 8.

**Alternatives** Other azaleas native to the eastern states that also produce fragrant flowers include Alabama azalea (*Rhododendron alabamense*), Zones 6 to 9; sweet azalea (*R. arborescens*), Zones 5 to 9; honeysuckle azalea (*R. canescens*), Zones 6 to 10; pinxterbloom azalea (*R. periclymenoides*, syn. *R. nudiflorum*); and swamp azalea (*R. viscosum*), both Zones 4 to 9.

## *Viola blanda* | Sweet White Violet
Perennial; 2 to 5 inches tall

No native woodland garden should be without at least one dainty violet, and this one is fragrant to boot. Sweet white violet is a small stoloniferous plant with pretty heart-shaped leaves. Each of its white flowers, which appear from early spring to early summer, rests atop its own reddish leafless stalk. It is native to moist woods from Newfoundland to Alberta, and from Maine to North Dakota, south to South Carolina, Georgia, and Alabama.

**Growing Tips** *Viola blanda* is easily grown in partial shade and moist, well-drained soil rich in organic matter. It spreads by runners to form large carpets. Zones 2 to 7.

**Alternatives** There are dozens of native violets, but sweet white violet reportedly is the most reliably fragrant.

# Scented Evening Gardens

Meghan Ray

Wouldn't it be great if all fragrant plants gave off their scent in a steady stream day and night so we could enjoy them whenever we pleased? Plants, however, have to operate under stricter rules of economy. Since plants use perfume to lure pollinators, and producing these scents uses up precious energy, many plants wait until their pollinators are active to release their fragrance. Moths emerge once the sun goes down, so flowers that count on these creatures of the night for reproductive services release their heady fragrances after sunset.

It is lucky for nighttime enthusiasts that moths prefer many of the same sweet scents that we like, making their flowers appealing choices for a garden that sends out its fragrance in the evening hours. The flowers of these plants are also predominantly white or light colored—easier for pollinators (and us) to see after dark. Unlike butterfly plants, which have nice landing areas on their flowers, moth-pollinated flowers tend to be tube or funnel shaped, specialized to accommodate the long, nectar-extracting proboscis (strawlike tongue) of a moth as it hovers.

The shrubs, vines, perennials, and annuals chosen for this evening patio all turn on their fragrance at night, and for this reason, their scents may not be familiar to many gardeners. The perfumes of these evening bloomers are mainly sweet, several with hints of lemon and almond.

In this design, hardy shrubs like deciduous sweet azalea (*Rhododendron arborescens*) and the evergreen holly osmanthus (*Osmanthus heterophyllus*) and Adam's needle (*Yucca filamentosa*) give the garden structure and texture year-round. The large-flowered angel's trumpet (*Brugmansia × candida*) and luxurious moonflower vine (*Ipomoea alba*) lend a lush, tropical effect during the warmer months. I have also interspersed annuals throughout the garden to ensure that fragrant flowers are in bloom from spring through summer.

Night-blooming flowers are perfect for extending the enjoyment of a garden beyond the daylight hours, especially for people whose activities often keep them away from their garden until after sunset. The predominately light-colored flowers seem to glow in the dusk, and as they release their scents into the evening air and attract fluttering nectar seekers, they create a multisensory delight.

**Thanks to light-colored flowers, silvery foliage, and intoxicating scents, this patio garden comes alive at dusk as moths swoop in for a visit.**

# A Scented Evening Garden

## DESIGN TIPS

- To maximize user-friendliness after dark, choose a level site; make paths, maybe using a light-reflecting material like gravel or oyster shells or light-colored pavers; and provide a source of light. Moonlight will illuminate the plants with a discreet glow, but candles, torches, or simple garden lights are a nice touch for moonless nights.

- Site the evening garden as near the house as possible to ensure easy access to plants that come to life at dusk, providing a reason to turn off the indoor electronics and venture out to enjoy the evening air.

- Include comfortable seating so that you and your friends and family will linger in the garden and drink in the scents.

- If space is limited, plant a container garden. The evening bloomers featured here can all thrive in pots on a terrace or balcony. See page 62 for more container garden tips.

## Plants Featured in This Garden

For a printer-friendly garden plan drawn to scale, visit bbg.org/fragrantdesigns.

1 *Brugmansia × candida,* angel's trumpet

2 *Hemerocallis citrina,* citron daylily

3 *Ipomoea alba,* moonflower

4 *Matthiola longipetala* subsp. *bicornis,* night stock

5 *Mirabilis longiflora,* sweet four o'clock

6 *Nicotiana × sanderae* 'Perfume Deep Purple', flowering tobacco

7 *Oenothera pallida,* pale evening primrose (not pictured)

8 *Osmanthus heterophyllus,* holly osmanthus

9 *Petunia hybrida,* petunia hybrids

10 *Rhododendron arborescens,* sweet azalea

11 *Yucca filamentosa,* Adam's needle (not pictured)

12 *Zaluzianskya capensis,* night phlox

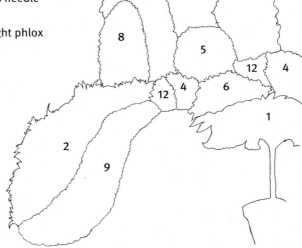

# Plants for a Scented Evening Garden

*All the plants featured here will thrive in regular garden soil, planted in full sun to partial shade, with regular watering during dry periods.*

## Brugmansia × candida
### Angel's Trumpet
Tender perennial shrub or tree; 5 to 10 feet tall

Angel's trumpet produces very showy flowers that release their sweet, lemony fragrance in the evening. It can bloom all year in a frost-free climate, but the heaviest bloom period is from summer through fall. The immense funnel-shaped flowers are white, pink, apricot, or yellow. Angel's trumpet can be pruned either as a shrub or as a small tree. The branches form a spreading canopy from which the flowers hang like fragrant bells. All parts of the plant are poisonous if ingested. Wash your hands after touching it.

**Growing Tips** In colder climates, grow angel's trumpet in a container and move it inside when temperatures fall below freezing. (Don't worry if the plant loses some leaves; it often becomes semideciduous in winter.) Keep it moist in summer and fertilize every two to three weeks with a balanced fertilizer (for example, NPK 3-3-3) but water only sparingly over the winter. Prune for shape and size in early spring. Zones 8 to 10.

**Alternatives** There are many fine cultivars. 'Double White' has, yes, double white flowers; 'Knightii' has double yellow flowers; 'Variegata' has cream-edged leaves and apricot flowers.

## Hemerocallis citrina
### Citron Daylily
Perennial; 3 to 4 feet tall

Daylilies are garden favorites with an enormous number of cultivars. Most flower in summer during July and August, and although each bloom reputedly lasts only one day, they are produced in such abundance that the flowering period can last for many weeks. The citron daylily has handsome dark green foliage and narrow, funnel shaped, light yellow blooms that open in the evening and release a powerful honeysuckle fragrance until the following morning.

**Growing Tips** Citron daylily is sturdy, long-lived, and requires little care once it is established. Every few years, divide the clumps to increase stock and maintain vigor. Zones 3 to 9.

**Alternatives** Despite attempts at hybrid crosses meant to generate fuller flowers and eliminate the plant's nocturnal habit—the resulting plants remained night blooming, and most of these crosses have been lost. Yellow-flowered *Hemerocallis* 'Hyperion' releases its sweet scent into the evening air; *H.* 'Zarahemla', another night-scented cultivar, displays pink flowers.

**Brugmansia × candida**, angel's trumpet

*Ipomoea alba*, moonflower

### *Ipomoea alba* | Moonflower

Tender perennial vine, widely grown as annual; 8 to 10 feet tall

*Ipomoea alba* probably originated in the New World tropics but is now found in wet forests and grasslands in many tropical regions around the globe. Grown from seed, the vine will bloom in the first year, and it can climb up to 10 feet in a single growing season. Lime-green heart-shaped leaves cover the twining stems, and the white flowers look like steroidal morning glories, measuring up to 6 inches across. The flowers unfurl so quickly at dusk that you can stand by and watch them open, and they emit a strong magnolia scent, lemony and sweet. The vine will flower abundantly from July to October.

**Growing Tips** Moonflower prefers well-drained sandy soil and full sun. Water during dry periods. The warmer it is, the faster it grows, making it a good summer screen. To start from seed, nick the seed coats and soak overnight to break dormancy. Before growing this plant where it is hardy, make sure it's not listed as invasive in your area (see www.invasive.org/weedus). Zones 10 to 12.

**Alternatives** *Passiflora incarnata*, maypop or purple passion flower, is native to the southeastern U.S. and hardy to Zone 5. Its striking, fragrant flowers appear from summer to fall, and its fruit can be eaten. In warm areas, maypop requires hard pruning to keep it in bounds.

### *Matthiola longipetala* subsp. *bicornis* | Night Stock
Annual; 20 inches tall

This unassuming native of southern Europe and Asia is slender, with narrow leaves and small, four-petaled flowers that range from white through pink to purplish brown. The flowers droop sadly by day, and the plant has a rather rangy habit, so it is best tucked away behind more substantial plants. Come evening, however, night stock makes up for all its daytime shortcomings. As darkness falls, the flowers open, and though still modest, they lose their forlorn appearance, filling the air with a strong, clean, spicy clove fragrance.

**Growing Tips** Night stock is very easy to grow from seed. Sow in place or start indoors and plant out once the weather gets warm. It

***Oenothera pallida*, pale evening primrose**

prefers sun but is not particular as to soil as long as it is well drained.

**Alternatives** *Matthiola incana* cultivars are the familiar garden stocks. Perennials often grown as annuals, they have a very spicy clove scent and come in colors ranging from white to dark purple. *Matthiola sinuata*, giant sea stock, is another evening-scented stock that grows on coastal dunes in England but is rarely cultivated in gardens.

## *Mirabilis longiflora*
## Sweet Four O'clock
Perennial; 5 feet tall

This perennial from the foothill canyons of the American Southwest and Mexico dies back to tuberous roots in colder climates. *Mirabilis longiflora* has a more sprawling habit than the common garden four o'clock (*M. jalapa*). The 6-inch-long white flowers have dark pink centers and curly magenta stamens and are very attractive to hawk moths. The flowers are closed during the day but open at dusk as temperatures cool down. Their fragrance is reminiscent of orange blossoms.

**Growing Tips** Sweet four o'clock can tolerate both full sun and partial shade. In colder areas, provide winter mulch or else lift the tubers, pack them in a plastic bag in vermiculite, and store them in a cool dry spot as you would dahlias. All parts of the plant are poisonous if ingested. Zones 7 to 11.

**Alternatives** *Mirabilis jalapa*, garden four o'clock, comes in a wide range of colors, and the intensity of fragrance varies in differrent cultivars.

## *Nicotiana* × *sanderae* 'Perfume Deep Purple' | Flowering Tobacco
Annual; 12 to 20 inches tall

Flowering tobacco is related to smoking tobacco and other members of the potato family. Many of the most commonly found ornamental cultivars of *Nicotiana* available today were selected from *N. alata* or the hybrid *N.* × *sanderae*. 'Perfume Deep Purple' has beautiful dark purple, upward-facing 2-inch flowers that stay open during the day but wait until nightfall to release their sweet scent. It blooms over a long period and is heat tolerant.

**Growing Tips** Sow seed indoors eight weeks before last frost, or buy plant starts and set them out once danger of frost has passed.

**Alternatives** The *Nicotiana × sanderae* 'Perfume' series also offers a color mix; *N. alata* 'Grandiflora' and 'Fragrant Cloud' are very fragrant, white-flowered forms; *N. sylvestris*, woodland tobacco, is a 5-foot-tall perennial in Zones 10 to 11, often grown as an annual. It is also strongly fragrant at night.

## *Oenothera pallida*
## Pale Evening Primrose
### Perennial; 8 to 20 inches tall

This member of the *Oenothera* clan is native to the western U.S. Pale evening primrose has bright green lance-shaped foliage and produces beautiful white flowers with pale yellow centers from early summer until autumn. They remain open during the day and are lightly scented. During the evening, the fresh sweet lemony scent that we know from their more common relative *O. biennis* becomes stronger and the flowers take on a luminosity perfect for the evening garden.

**Growing Tips** Pale evening primrose doesn't like wet feet and requires good drainage, especially in winter. Once established it can be quite drought tolerant. Avoid overly fertile soils, and cut back the foliage in the fall to maintain vigor. Zones 4 to 10.

**Alternatives** There are many species of evening primrose, including the yellow biennial common evening primrose, *Oenothera biennis*, and the pink evening primrose, *O. speciosa*. Many species are aggressive in the garden, so caveat emptor.

## *Osmanthus heterophyllus*
## Holly Osmanthus, Holly Olive
### Evergreen shrub; 10 feet tall

Native to evergreen forests of Japan and Taiwan, the dense upright habit and dark green foliage of holly osmanthus make it a

**Mirabilis longiflora, sweet four o'clock**

good structural element or screen in the garden. The small leaves are shaped like holly when young and become rounder with maturity. In fall this slow-growing plant is covered with small white flowers. The heavy, sweet fragrance is so strong that even in cool autumn weather it is carried far afield, enabling the curious to track it down from quite a distance.

**Growing Tips** Holly osmanthus prefers moist, well-drained acidic soil and a sunny situation. Plants can withstand heavy pruning. Zones 7 to 9.

**Alternatives** *Osmanthus heterophyllus* 'Goshiki' is a variegated cultivar of cream, gold, and green that needs some shade to prevent scorching; 'Variegatus' has creamy margins, less spiny leaves than the species, and does better in sun than 'Goshiki'. For less spiny foliage, try 'Rotundifolius', a slow-growing dwarf form with rounded leaves. It is somewhat less cold hardy than the species. The cultivar 'Gulftide' has glossy, bluish foliage and is very compact; it is more cold hardy than the species.

## *Petunia* hybrids
### Tender perennial, widely grown as annual; 6 to 18 inches tall

Most petunias sold today are complex hybrids of a few South American species, including *Petunia axillaris*, which is white-flowered and fragrant at night, and purple-blossomed *P. violacea*. The resulting hybrids have been divided into groups including multiflora, grandiflora, and cascading forms. The flowers have the funnel shape typical of the potato family, to which *Petunia* belongs, and range in size from 1 to 3½ inches long. At their best, the flowers have a pungent, spicy clove fragrance that is strongest at night.

**Growing Tips** When you pick up petunias at the nursery, look for plants in bloom and check them for scent. Many cultivars have some scent, but in my unscientific tests, purples and whites are always the most fragrant, and reds and yellows have little or no smell. Pinch back small plants bought in six packs right after transplanting to encourage bushy growth. Deadheading and light shearing can prolong bloom and maintain appearance. In warmer areas, make sure to get heat-tolerant cultivars. Zones 10 to 11.

**Alternatives** Cultivars come and go with new advances in breeding and rediscoveries of heirloom favorites. 'Midnight Madness' is a very dark purple multiflora type, as is 'Dreams Midnight Blue'.

## *Rhododendron arborescens*
## Sweet Azalea
### Deciduous shrub; 8 to 12 feet tall

Native to riversides and swamps across a large portion of the eastern U.S., sweet azalea has erect branches and glossy dark leaves. In early summer, after the leaves have fully expanded, flowers appear, usually in June and July. They emerge in groups of three to seven and are white to blush pink, with conspicuous red styles and stamens that make them seem even pinker. They smell very strongly and sweetly of almond, heliotrope, and cinnamon. The fragrance continues through the day into the evening. *Rhododendron arborescens* and many of its cultivars have crimson-red fall color.

**Growing Tips** Sweet azalea prefers well-drained, moist, acidic soil. It grows well in full sun to partial shade and needs little pruning. Zones 4 to 7.

**Alternatives** Cultivars include *Rhododendron arborescens* 'Dynamite' and 'Hot Ginger', both selected for strong fragrance. There are many more garden-worthy azaleas, but not many that are noted for evening fragrance.

## *Yucca filamentosa*
## Adam's Needle
### Evergreen shrub; 3 feet tall

Native to dry, sandy areas of the southeastern U.S., Adam's needle has a basal rosette of erect, spreading, swordlike foliage tipped with sharp spines. The stiff leaves make a good foil for less structural garden plants. In the summer, a 5- to 8-foot stalk bearing panicles of evening-scented, bell-shaped cream flowers rises from the foliage. By day, the bell-shaped flowers hang downward, but as night falls,

***Petunia*** **hybrid**

**Yucca filamentosa, Adam's needle**

the flowers turn upward and release their soapy fragrance into the night air to attract the plant's moth pollinator, *Tegeticula yuccasella*. The female moth collects pollen from one flower, forms it into a tight plug, and then flies on to the next flower. There she lays her eggs in the pistil and plugs the stigma with her pollen plug. The larvae that hatch have a safe, enclosed home, and the plug ensures the flower's pollination. Once they emerge, the larvae eat some (but not all) of the seeds, tunnel their way to freedom, and leave the rest of the flower's seeds to ripen. A tough and reliable plant, *Yucca filamentosa* adds drama with its tall flower stalks and architectural shape.

**Growing Tips** Tolerant of drought and poor soil as long as it is not excessively wet, yuccas are difficult to transplant due to their long taproot, so place with care when planting. Zones 4 to 9.

**Alternatives** There are many scented cultivars of *Yucca filamentosa*, including 'Bright Edge', which has leaves edged in yellow; 'Color Guard', with white-and-cream leaves with green margins; and 'Golden Sword',

which has green leaves with a yellow center. 'Blue Sword' is a blue-foliaged form.

## *Zaluzianskya capensis*
### Night Phlox
#### Annual; 12 to 18 inches tall

This South African native is covered with small flowers from July until fall. During the day, the bright green, fine-textured foliage is topped by tiny maroon balls. As the sun goes down, these open to reveal the white, phlox-like petals of the flowers. A few plants are enough to fill the evening garden with their very sweet, almond fragrance.

**Growing Tips** Sow seeds in place in the garden or start them indoors and plant out after danger of frost is past. Plant them in full sun except in the hottest areas. Deadhead the spent flowers for repeat bloom.

**Alternatives** *Silene nutans*, Nottingham catchfly, is a wildflower with pinkish-white blooms that grows on dry hillsides and in sandy soils in southeastern England and has a powerful scent that it releases in the evening. Zones 3 to 8.

# Aromatic Container Gardens
## Jennifer Williams

Fragrant plants and containers go naturally together. Fill a window box with small, seasonal sweet-perfumed gardenias, a pair of formal front-door containers with clipped fragrant tea olives, a strawberry jar on the kitchen patio with basil, oregano, and thyme, or a hanging planter with trailing tomatoes. Containers give gardeners options: You can fill them with specific soil mixes that suit particular plants; move them in and out of the sun if needed; water more or less depending on the plants' requirements; and move them indoors over the winter if the plants can't take the cold. They're also an invitation to be creative: Have fun playing with plant combinations, container styles, and how you arrange containers to define garden spaces, give privacy to a terrace, and hide or highlight a permanent feature.

## CONTAINER CULTIVATION TIPS

- Choose a pot: Anything that holds soil and allows drainage will work. Clay pots come in a variety of shapes and sizes and look better with age. However, they are porous, drying out quickly in summer and cracking in cold-winter climates as they absorb water that then freezes and expands. And like stone and concrete, they are heavy—good for stability, bad for portability. Though arguably less attractive, lighter, less expensive materials such as plastic, fiberglass, and metal are portable, hold moisture longer, and perfectly withstand cold winter weather.

- Make sure your pot has at least one hole in the bottom for drainage. Line the bottom of the container with a small piece of window-screen fabric to keep the soil in and let the water drain. Fill the pot with a sterile container mix (not garden soil) specific to your plants' needs. If making your own blend, add coarse material like poultry grit for drainage.

- If you have trouble keeping up with watering, add hydrogel granules to the soil blend before planting. They absorb many times their volume in water and release it slowly over time. Be sure to add the recommended amounts.

- Choose a color palette before you start, or base it on the colors of a specimen plant that will be the focal point of your container. Consider limiting it to colors that are either hot or cool. A cool palette might include plants with silver or white foliage and pastel flowers; a hot one might have deep purple and dark green foliage plants and scarlet, hot pink, and orange flowers.

**Versatile and creative, container gardens offer great opportunities for scent in small spaces.**

# Old-Fashioned, Low-Maintenance Planter

This informal grouping incorporates sweet-smelling, low-maintenance plants in a soft pastel color scheme of golden-chartreuse and green foliage and white and pink flowers that bloom from late spring through fall. The plants are complemented by the old-fashioned half-barrel container, which is roomy enough for them to prosper. This container measures 24 to 30 inches in diameter. Once planted, it will be too heavy and awkward to move easily, so place it with care.

## CULTIVATION TIPS

- When planting in a container assemble plants that have similar light, soil, and moisture requirements. The plants gathered here are all fairly resilient and drought tolerant, making the pot easy to maintain.

- Fill the container with a premixed commercial soil for shrubs and perennials. Add a bit of chicken grit to improve drainage and a slow-release fertilizer. Alternatively, mix a handfull of compost in with the potting soil at planting time.

- Plant the oriental lily bulbs first, and set them deeper than the other plants. A good rule of thumb is to plant bulbs three times the height of the bulb. Cover the bulbs with a thin layer of soil and set the two shrubs in the pot. Fill in with soil to 3 inches below their soil line. Next, place the anise hyssop and the annuals in the pot and fill up with soil to 3 inches below the rim of the pot. Place the container in full sun and water it well.

- This versatile container combines two hardy shrubs with a perennial herb, summer-flowering bulbs, and a few annuals. After the first frost, cover the soil with a 2-inch layer of mulch. Throughout winter, water the container when temperatures are above freezing and it seems dry. Once the weather warms in spring, remove dead foliage, look for seedlings of anise hyssop, dill, sweet alyssum, and four o'clocks, and continue watering the container as needed. Replace annuals as necessary.

## Plants Featured in This Container

1. *Agastache foeniculum* 'Golden Jubilee', anise hyssop
2. *Anethum graveolens* 'Hercules', dill
3. *Convallaria majalis* 'Aureovariegata', lily-of-the-valley
4. *Deutzia gracilis* 'Duncan' (CHARDONNAY PEARLS), slender deutzia (not pictured)
5. *Lilium* 'Le Reve', oriental lily
6. *Lobularia maritima* 'Carpet of Snow', sweet alyssum
7. *Mirabilis jalapa* 'Limelight', four o'clock
8. *Nicotiana alata*, jasmine tobacco
9. *Spartium junceum*, Spanish broom

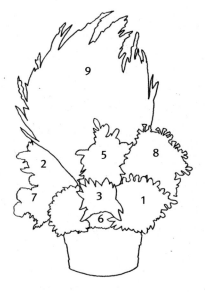

### Agastache foeniculum
### 'Golden Jubilee' | Anise Hyssop
Perennial; 20 inches tall

This easy-to-grow cultivar of a North American native has beautiful chartreuse-golden foliage, lavender-purple blooms, and a sweet, spicy, mint-licorice fragrance. From midsummer through the fall, the blooms attract bees and butterflies. Accustomed to dry, hilly habitats, this hyssop grows well in full sun and drier soils. Hardy to Zone 5.

### Anethum graveolens
### 'Hercules' | Dill
Annual; 36 inches tall

Native to India and southwestern Asia, dill has a uniquely pungent, tart aroma and flavor, best known as the main herb in pickled cucumbers. Very easy to grow, this lush herb displays blue-green, feathery leaves and airy chartreuse umbel flowers. It likes well-drained soils and full sun. Dill is a valuable food source for black and anise swallowtail butterfly larvae and attracts beneficial insects.

### Convallaria majalis
### 'Aureovariegata'
### Variegated Lily-of-the-Valley
Bulbous perennial; 12 inches tall

Lily-of-the-valley is known for its stunning and sweetly fragrant white bell-shaped flowers that abundantly appear throughout the late spring. On this cultivar, beautiful pinstripes mark the elliptically shaped foliage. The plant's broad evergreen leaves prefer shade to semishade, making it a perfect underplanting in a pot, where its spreading habit is neatly confined. Zones 3 to 7.

### Deutzia gracilis
### 'Duncan' (CHARDONNAY PEARLS)
### Slender Deutzia
Shrub; 2 to 3 feet tall and wide

This compact, heavy-blooming shrub tolerates full sun or partial shade and has scorch-resistant, serrated lime-yellow leaves. In mid-spring, buds resembling huge white pearls develop on cascading golden branches. By early summer, they open to become starry white, fragrant flowers that attract butterflies. Zones 5 to 8.

### Lilium 'Le Reve' | Oriental Lily
Bulbous perennial; 3 to 4 feet tall

This summer-blooming hybrid lily has lovely light pink blooms with lemon-yellow throats. Its intoxicatingly sweet perfume wafts through the garden in July and August. 'Le Reve' prefers full sun to partial shade and works well in larger containers; plant it at least 4 to 8 inches deep. Like many other lilies, it is a long-lasting, room-perfuming cut flower. Zones 3 to 8.

### Lobularia maritima
### 'Carpet of Snow' | Sweet Alyssum
Tender perennial, often grown as annual; 4 to 8 inches tall

See page 81.

**Deutzia gracilis** 'Duncan' (CHARDONNAY PEARLS), slender deutzia

*Agastache foeniculum*, 'Golden Jubilee' anise hyssop

### Mirabilis jalapa
### 'Limelight' | Four O'clock
Annual; 1 foot tall

This updated version of an old-fashioned cottage-garden favorite native to Peru and tropical areas of North and South America has fuchsia flowers with lime-green foliage. 'Limelight' is fast and easy to grow, likes full sun or partial shade, and flowers from mid-summer until frost. Masses of blooms with a sweet fragrance open in late afternoon and remain open all night for pollinators.

### Nicotiana alata
### Jasmine Tobacco
Tender perennial, often grown as annual; 5 feet tall

Also known as flowering tobacco, this old-fashioned heirloom from South America releases its heady fragrance in the evening hours to lure its nighttime pollinators. This somewhat short-lived but easy-to-grow plant displays long-lasting trumpet-shaped white flowers that smell of jasmine. The plants can grow to five feet and are known to self-sow. Cut back after flowering. Zones 10 to 11.

### Spartium junceum
### Spanish Broom
Evergreen shrub or small tree; 6 to 10 feet tall

This upright shrub native to the Mediterranean likes open sites, full sun, and well-drained soils. Its stringlike foliage recommends it as an accent or specimen plant, as does its incredible late-spring display of sweetly perfumed, bright yellow pealike flowers, which are followed by attractive downy pods. It is an invasive weed in California and should not be grown there. Zones 8 to 10.

## Mediterranean Summer Urn

A striking golden Italian cypress (*Cupressus sempervirens* 'Aurea') is the focal point of this seasonal container of drought-tolerant sun lovers. The narrow upright specimen plant is surrounded with much shorter aromatic and culinary herbs from the Mediterranean. The design mixes attractive leaf colors and textures, beautiful flowers, and intense fragrances. The Grecian clay urn reflects the style of the region and creates a dramatic and colorful display on any sunny patio or terrace. This design is for a container measuring between 18 and 24 inches in diameter.

# DESIGN AND CULTIVATION TIPS

- The size of the cypress tree's root-ball will dictate the size of the container (18 to 24 inches in diameter). If the planting is permanent or intended to last more than a few seasons, use a pot that can accommodate root growth for at least several years.

- Scale, proportion, and balance are critical. The cypress should be three to five times the height of the perennials so that the herbs wrap around the base of the tree.

- All the plants are adapted to hot and dry conditions, so they prefer full sun and good drainage. In a mild climate where the temperature never drops below 35°F, the container can stay outside year-round. In colder areas, treat it as a seasonal display and move into a greenhouse (if available) for the colder months or place it in a sheltered spot. If you choose an alternative conifer (see *Cupressus sempervirens*, next page) adapted to cold weather, your pot can stay outdoors over the winter.

- Fill the container with a premixed commercial soil for shrubs and perennials. Add a bit of chicken grit (crushed granite), vermiculite, or even a small bag of a desert or cactus dry soil mix to assure excellent drainage, a must for these plants.

- Add a slow-release granular fertilizer (NPK 20-20-20) to provide nutrients for six to eight months. Mix the recommended amount into the soil before planting. In following years sprinkle fertilizer on the soil surface in spring and gently work it into the top of the soil.

- Plant the cypress first. Score its root-ball with a knife or pruners, put some soil in the bottom of the container, then center the tree in the pot so that its soil line is about three inches below the rim. Fill the pot with soil to 3 inches below the tree's soil line. Add the perennial herbs, spacing them evenly around the container to give them adequate growing space. Continue filling with soil to 3 inches below the rim. Every now and then rap the pot firmly on the sides to settle the soil. Place the container in full sun and water deeply. Water well when the top inch of soil is dry.

## Plants Featured in This Container

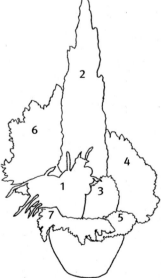

1    *Allium sativum* var. *ophioscorodon,* serpent garlic

2    *Cupressus sempervirens* 'Aurea', Italian cypress

3    *Lavandula stoechas* 'Lemon Leigh', lemon lavender

4    *Nepeta* × *faassenii* 'Six Hills Giant', catmint

5    *Origanum vulgare* 'Aureum', golden creeping oregano

6    *Perovskia atriplicifolia* 'Little Spire', Russian sage

7    *Rosmarinus officinalis* 'Prostratus', creeping rosemary

## Allium sativum var. ophioscorodon
### Serpent Garlic
Perennial; 2 feet tall

Serpent garlic, a member of the onion family, grows well in cooler weather. The plant's common name comes from its interestingly coiled flowering stems. Plant it in fall or earliest spring from a set; white to pink flowers appear in late spring to early summer. Both the cut stems and the bulbs are pungently aromatic. Zones 3 to 9.

## Cupressus sempervirens 'Aurea'
### Golden Italian Cypress
Coniferous tree; up to 15 feet tall

*Cupressus sempervirens* is a narrowly columnar conifer from the Mediterranean that can grow to 100 feet, but the cultivar 'Aurea' grows to only 12 to 15 feet and displays beautiful bright scalelike leaves that are chartreuse instead of the usual blue green. In a container its roots are restricted, so it will be even smaller. It has a surprisingly lemony scent that is quite strong when the needles are crushed. The tree

**Allium sativum var. ophioscorodon,**
serpent garlic

performs best in Zones 8 to 10 and needs winter protection from cold, drying winds.

**Alternatives** Fragrant alternatives for colder areas include hollywood juniper (*Juniperus chinensis* 'Kaizuka'), Zones 3 to 9, and 'Skyrocket' juniper (*J. scopularum* 'Skyrocket'). Zones 4 to 9.

## Lavandula stoechas
### 'Lemon Leigh' | Lemon Lavender
Perennial; 1 foot tall

Unlike most lavenders, lemon lavender has pale yellow to chartreuse, pineapple-shaped blooms that appear in late spring to early summer. This cultivar has the species' aromatic bluish-gray foliage and bushy habit. Zones 8 to 9.

## Nepeta × faassenii
### 'Six Hills Giant' | Catmint
Perennial; 3 feet tall

'Six Hills Giant' catmint has aromatic soft, hairy, silvery gray-green leaves and bears numerous spikes of lavender-blue flowers from late spring through fall, attracting butterflies, bees, and the occasional hummingbird. Shear this clump-forming plant by a third after its initial flowering to encourage a second, late-summer bloom. Zones 4 to 8.

## Origanum vulgare 'Aureum'
### Golden Creeping Oregano
Perennial; 4 inches tall

Golden oregano, from mountainous regions of the Mediterranean and southwestern Asia, is a spreading plant with beautiful oval, chartreuse leaves and the typical oregano scent. Its pink flowers in midsummer are popular with insect pollinators. This rhizomatous perennial is perfect as an underplanting or cascading over a container's edge. Oregano prefers full sun, but light afternoon shade may help keep the golden leaves from scorching. Zones 5 to 9.

**Nepeta × faassenii 'Six Hills Giant', catmint**

### Perovskia atriplicifolia
### 'Little Spire' | Russian Sage
**Semiwoody shrub; 2 to 3 feet tall**

This aromatic, easy-to-grow woody shrub originates in rocky sites from Central Asia to the Himalayas. The cultivar 'Little Spire', an upright, multistemmed clumper, tolerates dry coastal conditions and blooms midsummer through fall. Its finely cut, soft gray-green leaves have the heavy, pungent scent typical of sages. Each stem is topped with violet-blue flower panicles. In full bloom, the plant looks like a misty silvery-purple haze. 'Little Spire' is shorter than the species. Zones 5 to 9.

### Rosmarinus officinalis
### 'Prostratus' | Creeping Rosemary
**Tender perennial; 10 inches**

This small evergreen shrub has leathery, linear dark green leaves with silvery undersides and a sharp pinelike fragrance. Intense cobalt-purple blooms appear from mid-spring through early summer. This low-growing spreader is quite different from the upright species and is perfect for sunny walls or for spilling over the sides of containers. Hardy in Zones 8 to 10.

## Thai Coconut Curry Container

Designed around the scents of a wonderful Thai curry, this container is filled
with a lush, informal, yet dramatic mix of sun-loving plants evoking a sense of
the smells of Southeast Asian cuisine—as well as a few of its flavors. Leaf colors
range from chartreuse to maroon and flower colors from pink to scarlet. The focal
points—large, bold green-and-gold variegated ginger leaves and strikingly thin,
tall blades of lemongrass—are complemented by the feathery, spiky, and soft
textures of the other plants. This container is at its best in late summer, when
the plants are full and the tomato vine is fruiting. The container should measure
20 to 24 inches in diameter.

# CULTIVATION TIPS

- Fill the container with a commercial mix for flowering plants and vegetables and add slow-release fertilizer pellets (NPK 20-20-20) to supplement nutrients for six to eight months. You can also add an organic fertilizer such as composted manure (purchased in bags). Whatever you choose, apply it in moderation to avoid burning the plants.

- Because it prefers consistently moist soil, plant the tropical ginger in its own smaller pot with a heavier mix and more organic material like mushroom compost or bark; nestle the plant in its pot into the large container. When the weather cools in fall, take the ginger pot out and move it to a well-lit spot indoors, keeping the temperature above 65°F. Keep the soil evenly moist and mist often through the winter.

- Mix a small amount of chicken grit into the soil where you are planting curry plant, lemon grass, and scented geranium, as these three prefer a faster-draining medium.

- Water the container whenever the first half-inch or so of soil feels dry; check daily in summer. Water thoroughly using a gentle spray nozzle until water runs out through the drainage hole.

- Pinch back the pineapple sage and lemon balm in early summer to about 5 or 6 inches to encourage bushy plants with more flowers. Trim cilantro and chives frequently with scissors; cut them to the base to promote new growth, which is more flavorful and aromatic. Pinch basil foliage back throughout the summer to prevent flowering. The blooms are quite attractive and fragrant, but flowering makes the leaves become bitter.

- Before the first frost, move the ginger and lemon grass indoors, and cut the other perennials back to 3 or 4 inches above the soil line. If available, place the container in a sheltered spot protected from the wind and cover with evergreen boughs. When the weather is above freezing, check the container, and if the soil feels dry, water it.

## Plants Featured in This Container

1  *Allium tuberosum*, oriental chives
2  *Alpinia zerumbet* 'Variegata', variegated ginger
3  *Coriandrum sativum*, cilantro, coriander
4  *Cymbopogon citratus*, lemongrass
5  *Helichrysum italicum* subsp. *microphyllum*, miniature curry plant (not pictured)
6  *Lycopersicon esculentum* var. *cerasiforme* 'Tumbling Tom Yellow', tomato
7  *Melissa officinalis* 'Lime', lemon balm
8  *Ocimum basilicum* 'Siam Queen', Thai basil
9  *Pelargonium grossularioides*, coconut-scented geranium (not pictured)
10  *Salvia elegans* 'Golden Delicious', pineapple sage

### Allium tuberosum
### Oriental Chives
Bulbous perennial; 12 to 18 inches tall

This fast and easy-growing perennial from Southeast Asia has linear, dark green leaves that are more strongly flavored than those of common chives and are sometimes used as a mild substitute for raw garlic—but they also look beautiful in the garden when flowering. Oriental chives bear many star-shaped, fragrant white umbels throughout the summer. Take note that this is a vigorous self-sower. Zones 3 to 9.

### Alpinia zerumbet 'Variegata'
### Variegated Ginger
Tender perennial; 3 feet tall

Also known as shell ginger or pink porcelain lily, this cultivar's striking upright foliage striped in dark green and pale yellow has a slight scent of ginger and adds flair to summer containers. In late summer, pale pinkish-white fragrant flowers resembling seashells appear. Move it indoors when temperatures fall below 65°F at night. Zones 9 to 10.

**Alpinia zerumbet 'Variegata',
variegated ginger**

### Coriandrum sativum
### Cilantro, Coriander
Annual; 10 inches tall

This aromatic culinary herb, a staple in Thai cuisine, has bright green, feathery-tipped, parsleylike leaves. Some find the flavor and scent refreshing, lemony, and light; others find it metallic, soapy, and pungent. To grow it for its leaves, site it in partial shade to prevent bolting. Keep the soil evenly moist and harvest regularly with scissors to encourage tender new growth.

### Cymbopogon citratus
### Lemongrass
Tender perennial; 3 feet tall

Well known because of its place in Asian cuisine, especially Thai, this aromatic grass of tropical and subtropical southern India and Sri Lanka has long, hollow, canelike stems and narrow, pale blue-green blades strongly redolent of lemon. At summer's end, cut it back to three inches and move it indoors for the winter, and return it outside in late spring. Zones 8 to 10.

### Helichrysum italicum
### subsp. *microphyllum*
### Miniature Curry Plant
Tender perennial; 1 foot tall

Native to sunny slopes in Turkey, curry plant is an intensely aromatic, compact evergreen with woolly stems and linear, silver-gray to yellowish-green leaves and dark yellow flowers in late summer. When the leaves are cut or crushed, they smell strongly of curry. Zones 7 to 10.

### Lycopersicon esculentum
### 'Tumbling Tom Yellow' | Tomato
Tender perennial, often grown as annual; 2 feet tall

This easy-to-grow tomato has beautiful bright golden-yellow, cherry-sized fruits that are deliciously sweet. Both foliage and fruit

*Helichrysum italicum* **subsp.** *microphyllum*, **miniature curry plant**

have a weeping habit that allow the plant to drape over the sides of containers, window boxes, or hanging baskets. It needs full sun to fruit properly.

### *Melissa officinalis* 'Lime'
### Lemon Balm
Perennial; 2 feet tall

A native of southern Europe, lemon balm is a decorative, drought-tolerant plant. It prefers full sun to partial shade and produces fuzzy, light green, whorled leaves similar to mint. This cultivar has a strong smell of lime. The pale yellow flowers bloom sporadically throughout the summer and attract bees and butterflies. Pinch the stems back in spring to produce a bushier plant. Zones 4 to 9.

### *Ocimum basilicum*
### 'Siam Queen' | Basil
Annual; 1 foot tall

'Siam Queen' has interesting colors—the narrow leaves are green and purple, and the flowers are a striking burgundy—a pungent scent of licorice and clove, and a spicy flavor. Pinch back the plant to make it bushy.

### *Pelargonium grossularioides*
### Coconut-Scented Geranium
Tender perennial; 10 inches tall

Like other scented geraniums, this coconut scented cultivar is mostly grown for its aromatic deep green foliage rather than its magenta flowers. It prefers full sun but will tolerate partial shade, especially in the heat of the day. To prevent legginess, pinch back stems. Deadheading spent flowers promptly will encourage new shoots. Overwinter this geranium as a houseplant on a sunny windowsill. Zones 9 to 11.

### *Salvia elegans* 'Golden
### Delicious' | Pineapple Sage
Tender perennial; 3 feet tall

'Golden Delicious' is a bright golden, pineapple-scented sage cultivar that needs a bit of afternoon shade to keep its brilliant leaves from scorching. The scarlet-red flowers attract bees, butterflies, and hummingbirds from late August into fall. Zones 7 to 11.

# Fragrant Gardens for Children
## Monika Hannemann

A garden is a natural playground and living laboratory, where children can discover, explore, play, build, imagine, grow, create, and wonder. In a garden profuse with plant textures, colors, flavors—and especially scents—they will be curious, inspired, and involved. Given the chance to use their senses to connect with plants, kids can develop a deep relationship with nature that will last their lifetime.

The garden plan featured here highlights plants that are particularly effective at engaging young scientists and gardeners. Most of the plants are easy to start from seed, grow quickly, and don't require a lot of care. As kids raise plants from seeds and see the results of their labor, they will develop a sense of ownership and pride. When birds, bees, butterflies, and other wildlife flock to their garden turned living laboratory, children will learn firsthand about pollination, plant reproduction, and ecology. Invite the children to listen, smell, and watch. Along the way, explain to small children when it is okay to touch or taste and when to check with an adult first.

This sample garden is about 16 feet long by 8 feet wide—large enough for small groups of children to gather around the raised beds and planters, but small enough to feel cozy and intimate and so that kids are surrounded on all sides by plants. As they walk around the beds, children can get close enough to smell the flowers and gently rub leaves and stems to release their aromas, experiencing a range of scents from spicy to sweet, musky to fruity. Most of the plants here start performing in early spring and end in late fall—many, such as French marigold (*Tagetes patula*) and pineapple sage (*Salvia elegans*), are interesting to touch and smell throughout the growing season, flowering or not.

Sensory gardens like this one create opportunities for hands-on inquiries, explorations, and experiments. Many of these plants are herbs and are edible or useful in other ways—for perfume, potpourri, or other crafts. Children and adults are encouraged to discover creative ways to use the plants that they grow throughout the year.

**Beds raised 2 to 3 feet above ground level bring plants within easy reach of small hands and noses and keep them safe from the feet of enthusiastic young gardeners.**

# A Fragrant Garden for Children

# DESIGN AND CULTIVATION TIPS

- Choose plants for your children's garden that, like the plants here, are wildlife-friendly and attractive to the local birds, bees, hummingbirds, and butterflies. Kids love to watch animals, and they will be able to observe many creatures at work, interacting with the plants.

- Grow plants in containers and raised beds so that kids can reach the plants from all sides. In this garden, the soil level of the beds is 2 to 3 feet above the ground, and the beds are just 2 feet wide for easy access from either side. The space between beds is 4 feet, wide enough to bring in a wheelbarrow or garden cart.

- If using pots, make sure the containers are at least 16 to 20 inches in diameter and have drainage holes. Use a soil mix that's a 4 to 1 ratio of indoor potting mix to finished garden compost, or make your own soil blend from compost, coir dust, and coarse sand. Let the kids mix the soil components together—this is an essential part of the gardening process.

- Site your garden so that all the plants get full sun—or at the very least three to four hours—and monitor them regularly to see if they need water.

- The lightweight movable wooden benches at either end of the garden serve many purposes. They can contain the children in the garden. They also provide a spot where children can sit to examine a plant part more closely or participate in an activity. They can also serve as tables for plant explorations and crafts, and smaller children can stand on them to get easier access to the planting beds.

- A 3- to 4-inch layer of shredded wood mulch makes a soft but resilient, water-permeable and weed-suppressing ground covering for the center of the garden.

## Plants Featured in This Garden

For a printer-friendly garden plan drawn to scale, go to bbg.org/fragrantdesigns.

1  *Aloysia citriodora*, lemon verbena
2  *Dolichos lablab*, hyacinth bean vine
3  *Heliotropium arborescens*, heliotrope
4  *Lobularia maritima*, alyssum
5  *Mentha × piperita* 'Chocolate', chocolate mint
6  *Muscari armeniacum*, grape hyacinth (not pictured)
7  *Narcissus jonquilla*, dwarf jonquil (not pictured)
8  *Pelargonium fragrans*, nutmeg-scented geranium
9  *Salvia elegans*, pineapple sage
10  *Senna* (syn. *Cassia*) *didymobotrya*, popcorn senna
11  *Tagetes patula*, French marigold
12  *Viola tricolor*, Johnny jump-up

# Plants for a Fragrant Garden for Children

## *Aloysia citriodora*
## Lemon Verbena
Tender shrub; 6 feet tall

Rub lemon verbena's crinkly green leaves to release the refreshing, clean fragrance of the "queen of lemons," praised for the purity of its scent. Lemon verbena leaves are used for herbal teas, in potpourri, and to flavor fish and poultry dishes. They are sometimes rubbed on skin to keep bugs away. The shrub has white or purple flowers in June or July, but these are unscented.

**Growing Tips** Lemon verbena can be propagated from softwood cuttings but is most often purchased as a small plant from a garden center. It does best in dry, sandy soil. Try overwintering it indoors. It may drop its leaves at first but should recover in time. Zones 8 to 11.

**Alternatives** Other great lemon-scented plants include lemon balm (*Melissa officinalis*, page 71), lemongrass (*Cymbopogon citratus*, page 70), and lemon basil.

## *Dolichos lablab*
## Hyacinth bean vine
Tender perennial vine, often grown as annual; 30 feet tall

This Asian vine is a member of the bean family and is related to other legumes, including peas and beans. It has three-part dark green leaves. Stems and leaf undersides are purple, creating an interesting color contrast. Purple clusters of flowers with a soft, sweet scent appear in midsummer. These are magnets for butterflies and hummingbirds. The flowers yield to bright maroon seedpods in early fall. Invite kids to pick them and check out the beans inside—and save some for planting the following spring.

**Growing Tips** Hyacinth bean's large black-and-white seeds are easy to germinate in a damp paper towel. Planted in well-drained, fertile soil in late spring, the seeds will sprout in a week to ten days. Hyacinth bean vine grows well in full sun and is great to train up obelisks, trellises, and arches. Zones 8 to 10.

**Alternatives** *Dolichos lablab* 'Ruby Moon' has bicolor flowers of pink and purple. Other colorful, fragrant vines include 'Little Sweetheart' sweet pea (*Lathyrus odoratus*), with a powerful sugary-sweet flower scent, and scarlet runner bean (*Phaseolus coccineus*) and nasturtium (*Tropaeolum majus*), which have spicy-smelling flowers.

## *Heliotropium arborescens*
## Heliotrope
Tender perennial subshrub, often grown as annual; 15 to 20 inches tall

Heliotrope's purple flower clusters smell delicious—like cherry pie, almond, and vanilla. This tropical from South America, grown as an annual in most North American gardens, has sandpapery leaves and a gnarly

***Dolichos lablab*, hyacinth bean vine**

*Heliotropium arborescens*, heliotrope

shape. It blooms nonstop throughout the summer, making it a worthwhile addition to any fragrance garden. The flower nectar is popular with insect pollinators like bees, butterflies, and moths. Watch these plants carefully; the leaves actually turn toward the sun (its name is derived from the Greek *helios* for "sun" and *tropein* for "to turn"). The plant is grown commercially in southern Europe to make perfume.

**Growing Tips** Buy small plants or start heliotrope seeds indoors a few weeks before the last frost date, then transplant the seedlings into the garden once the soil has warmed. Zones 9 to 11.

**Alternatives** Cultivars include *Heliotropium arborescens* 'Album', 'Marine', and 'Dwarf Marine'. All have flowers that smell like cherry pie. Kid-friendly relatives include sweetly fragrant forget-me-nots (*Myosotis sylvatica*), which smell strongest at night, and Virginia bluebells (*Mertensia virginica*), which quickly emerge in early spring to flower with a delicately sweet scent and then go dormant and completely vanish from the scene within a few short weeks.

## *Lobularia maritima*
## Sweet Alyssum

**Tender perennial, often grown as annual; 4 to 8 inches tall**

Sweet alyssum bears dense clusters of tiny honey-scented pink, purple, or white flowers continuously from spring to fall. (White flowers are said to have the strongest fragrance, but test this for yourself.) Plant them with strawberries (*Fragaria* species, page 105) in a strawberry pot and watch out for bees and butterflies. This well-loved member of the Brassicaceae is related to mustards and broccoli (but has a much sweeter scent).

**Growing Tips** It's easy to grow this maintenance-free edging plant from seed. Thin seedlings to about 6 inches apart to form a groundcover, or plant it in containers or between pavers. Pinch back spent blooms to encourage flowers throughout the summer. Zones 7 to 10.

**Alternatives** *Lobularia maritima* 'Lilac Queen' and 'Royal Carpet' have purple flowers, 'Carpet of Snow' and 'Snow Crystals' are dwarf forms with masses of white flowers.

*Muscari armeniacum,* **grape hyacinth**

### *Mentha × piperita* 'Chocolate' Chocolate Mint
Perennial; 20 inches tall

Chocolate mint is a member of the bustling mint family—including peppermint, lavender, and rosemary, which all show their family association by their square stems. Chocolate mint is a spreading perennial groundcover with smooth green and bronze leaves. When rubbed, the leaves give off the heady chocolate-mint aroma for which the plant is named. The flowers are also minty.

**Growing Tips** Like other mints, chocolate mint grows very aggressively in well-drained soil in sun to partial shade. Always plant it in containers—never in the ground—to keep it under control. Harvest the leaves and stems often to keep it contained and bushy—add them to drinks and desserts. Grow new plants by taking stem cuttings—new roots will grow from the stems within a week in either soil or water. Zones 3 to 9.

**Alternatives** Try tangy-leafed lemon balm (*Melissa officinalis,* page 71) or orange mint (*Mentha × piperita* f. *citrata*).

### *Muscari armeniacum* Grape Hyacinth
Perennial; 10 inches tall

The flowers or these aptly named bulbs are clusters of small, downward-facing bells resembling grapes, which also smell like sweet grape juice. They flower for about three weeks in mid- to late spring. Grape hyacinths are originally from Eurasia and are cousins of onions and lilies.

**Growing Tips** Plant bulbs in small groups 3 inches deep in the fall; they will bloom the following spring and for many springs thereafter. Propagate by separating bulb offsets. Zones 4 to 8.

**Alternatives** *Muscari armeniacum* 'Album' is white but less fragrant than the species. *M. latifolium* has wider leaves and light blue to blue-black flowers and is intensely fragrant. Showy hyacinth (*Hyacinthus orientalis*) is larger, to 12 inches, comes in many colors, and boasts an even stronger sweet scent than grape hyacinths.

## Narcissus jonquilla
### Dwarf Jonquil
Perennial; 6 to 8 inches tall

Jonquils are small daffodils that produce freshly sweet flowers that are smaller and flatter than full-sized daffs and have multiple flowers per stem—generally 2 to 6 blossoms each. The flowers may be yellow, orange, white, or a combination of all three. Daffodils, members of the lily family, are related to tulips, onions, and garlic.

**Growing Tips** Plant the bulbs in fall for blooms the following spring. They will naturalize over time if the foliage is not mowed but rather allowed to die back naturally. Otherwise propagate jonquils by dividing the bulbs once the flowers and leaves have died back. Zones 3 to 9.

**Alternatives** Fun miniature cultivars with slightly less fragrant but adorable 2- to 4-inch flowers include *Narcissus jonquilla* 'Baby Moon', 'Kidling', and 'Suzy'. Especially fragrant cultivars include 'Fruit Cup', 'Fragrant Rose', and 'Martinette'; their flowers smell like gardenia mixed with orange blossom—pungent!

## Pelargonium fragrans
### Nutmeg-Scented Geranium
Tender perennial; 12 to 20 inches tall

This plant's energizing, nutmeg-spicy leaves are small and have a velvety-soft, smooth texture. It is sometimes called the scratch 'n' sniff plant: Touch the leaves all you like; it thrives with handling. Nutmeg-scented geranium sprawls in mounds in beds and over containers during the growing season, but in cold-winter climates it will die after frost unless brought inside. Small pink and white flowers appear in spring and early summer. These are edible but less fragrant than the leaves.

**Growing Tips** Scented geraniums are easy to grow from stem cuttings (in water and soil). Cut plants back in fall and move them inside as houseplants. Keep them fairly dry. Zones 8 to 11.

**Alternatives** Various cultivars have leaf scents reminiscent of rose, apple, lemon, apricot, coconut, ginger, and more. Favorites are 'Pungent Peppermint' and 'Roses of Attar'. Cuban oregano (*Plectranthus amboinicus*) is similar in size but boasts intense, oregano-scented leaves.

## Salvia elegans | Pineapple Sage
Tender perennial, often grown as annual; 5 feet tall

This member of the mint family is native to the Mediterranean and South America. The soft, fuzzy leaves smell like pineapple when rubbed; their fresh tropical-paradise scent can make your mouth water. The plant will surprise you in early fall with brilliant red tubular flowers, which attract hummingbirds. Combine pineapple sage and lemon verbena leaves to make a delicious fruity tea.

**Growing Tips** Plant pineapple sage in full sun and give it plenty of space for its branches to spread. Propagate by taking stem

***Salvia elegans*, pineapple sage**

cuttings from tips of mature stems. Root these quickly in water, then transplant into soil. Pineapple sage is grown as an annual in cooler regions. Zones 9 to 11.

**Alternatives** *Salvia elegans* 'Wild Watermelon' has fruity bubblegum-scented leaves, and 'Frieda Dixon', a dwarf cultivar, has salmon flowers and pineapple-scented foliage. Maraschino cherry salvia (*S. grahamii* × *microphylla*) has fresh, fruit-scented leaves, Also try tricolor sage (*S. officinalis* 'Tricolor') and Mexican sage (*S. leucantha*).

## Senna (syn. Cassia) didymobotrya | Popcorn Senna
Tender shrub; 10 feet tall

Popcorn senna, a tender shrub native to tropical east Africa, has intensely fragrant feathery leaves that release the scent of buttered popcorn when they are scratched or crushed. It is quick-growing and can grow 7 to 12 feet tall in full sun in one season. Butter-colored flower spikes form in July and August, but they are not particularly fragrant. Popcorn senna, a member of the bean family, is related to sensitive plant

(*Mimosa pudica*), and like that plant, its leaves fold up at night and open during the day. Plant it with peppermint-patty-scented chocolate mint (see above) for the complete movie-theater sensory experience!

**Growing Tips** Start popcorn senna from seeds, which germinate quickly, or take woody stem cuttings from mature plant tips. Take the plant inside in fall and keep it in a sunny window. Drought-tolerant popcorn senna is still somewhat new to the nursery trade but is becoming more available as its popularity grows. Zones 9 to 11.

**Alternatives** Perennial lupine (*Lupinus perennis*) has honey-scented flowers; biennial evening primrose (*Oenothera* species, page 59) has jasmine-scented flowers; and annual stock (*Matthiola incana*) has spicy clove-scented flowers.

## Tagetes patula | French Marigold
Annual; 6 to 12 inches tall

Marigolds bloom all summer long and bring brightness and cheer to any garden; they are also fun to cut for bouquets. French marigolds have pinnate green leaves and form small bushy mounds. Their flowers may be yellow, white, orange, or red (or a combination). Reviews are mixed about their pungent musky odor, which remind some people of moist soil. The scent comes from the chemical terpene, which is often said to keep insects, deer, and rabbits away from the garden. They are native to the southwestern U.S. and South America, and along with zinnias and sunflowers, they belong to the daisy family.

**Growing Tips** Marigolds are among the easiest and most rewarding plants to start from seed—a great project for young children. In the garden, pluck fading blooms to keep new ones coming—crush the old flowers in your hand to collect new marigold seeds. When they dry, plant them in fresh soil to start the growing cycle all over again. In fall, save seeds for the following year.

***Senna didymobotrya*, popcorn senna**

*Viola tricolor*, **johnny jump-up**

**Alternatives** Some favorite cultivars include multicolored *Tagetes patula* 'Pinwheel', 'Safari', and vibrantly colored 'Disco'. Dwarf-sized signet marigolds (*T. tenuifolia*) such as 'Lemon Gem' and 'Tangerine Gem' (page 40) have tangy, citrus-scented *and* flavored flowers—they're delicious! A nonedible alternative is the petunia (*Petunia* hybrids, page 60), with mildly sweet-scented flowers.

## *Viola tricolor* | Johnny Jump-up
**Perennial, often grown as annual; 6 inches tall**

Get up close to these cheerful multicolored flowers to discover their expressive faces. The flowers are edible and come in combinations of purple, orange, yellow, and white. They are members of the violet family, which includes wild violet species (native to Europe and North America) as well as garden pansies. Most are perennial, but many are grown as annuals in cold-winter climates. They have heart-shaped or oval leaves, and their flowers have a sweet, delicate perfume. Johnny jump-ups are said to be more fragrant at dawn and dusk than midday.

**Growing Tips** Plants can be started from seed, but it's easiest to purchase them as sets from garden centers in spring or fall. Plant them close together to concentrate their fragrance, and deadhead flowers regularly for continuous bloom. They flower best during the cooler weather of spring and fall. They self-seed easily. Zones 4 to 8.

**Alternatives** *Viola tricolor* 'Etain', 'The Czar', and 'Starry Night' are very fragrant. Other scented relatives include the sweet violets *V. odorata* 'Rosea' and 'Eastgrove Blue Scented' (which smells like lilacs). Pansy relatives (*V.* × *wittrockiana*) often have larger, expressive faces and come in a variety of color patterns but have only subtly fragrant flowers.

# Scented Paths
## Caleb Leech

Fragrance is one of the most powerful tools at the gardener's disposal. More than any of the other senses, smell is most closely allied with memory. Even the mere hint of a scent—be it as subtle as that of woodland fern or as pungent as a tomato's leaves—can evoke a long-forgotten experience. Cultivate fragrant plants along a path, and you will cast an aromatic spell over all who pass.

Paths may well be the most important feature in a garden. They separate the garden into different zones, connect the back door to an outdoor sitting area, lead the eye toward a special plant or other garden feature, and invite visitors to take a leisurely stroll from one area of interest to another. Bordered with plants that release their fragrances at different times of the day or evening or when their foliage is brushed or trod on, the practical garden path becomes sublime.

Most of the fragrant plants in the design presented here were selected with an eye to easy cultivation, with long-lived, low-maintenance shrubs and perennials combined with self-sowing annuals. Delicate ferns emerge in early spring to blanket the ground, and upright grasses and sages provide four-season interest and vertical accents in the garden. Self-sowing annuals such as fern-leaf lavender (*Lavandula multifida*), holy basil (*Ocimum sanctum*), and even tomatoes (*Lycopersicon esculentum*) give the gardener the opportunity to strike a balance between spontaneity and formality. Plants that spring up between the paving stones may be clipped back, transplanted, trellised, or allowed to remain in place for a more wild, informal look.

The aromatic foliage of peppermint geranium (*Pelargonium tomentosum*) and ornamental oregano (*Origanum laevigatum*) spills out from the border onto the walkway, rewarding strollers with a rich palette of scents as they brush by. Chamomile (*Anthemis nobilis*) creeps between the pavers, offering a profusion of daisylike spring flowers and an apple fragrance wafting up from underfoot. Later in the season, chocolate flower (*Berlandiera lyrata*) fills the morning air with a delightful, mouthwatering chocolate aroma. As the smell of chocolate wanes in the warmth of the afternoon, the licorice fragrance of holy basil entices the senses. Be it morning, noon, or evening, the path's contrasting foliage textures and lively color combinations of silver, gray, and purple hues set off against emerald and lime greens lure visitors to indulge all their senses.

**Allow plants with fragrant foliage to reach out over the edges of the path so they release their scents as passersby brush against them.**

# A Scented Path

# DESIGN AND CULTIVATION TIPS

- When choosing a material for pavers, if you use them at all, look for locally quarried or salvaged stone. Their irregular shapes are attractive interplanted with fragrant herbs and groundcovers. Lay the stone on a base grade of crushed granite or similar material. Fill the spaces between the stones with a soil mixture containing at least 25 percent coarse sand or grit to create a growing medium suitable for many herbs and wildflowers that require excellent drainage and a lean substrate.

- Plant rugged, mat-forming herbs like chamomile, Corsican mint, or pennyroyal between the pavers. The sun will warm the stones, and the extra heat will make the plants' fragrant essential oils more noticeable as visitors tread the path.

- Vary the pathside plantings to suit the existing landscape and light conditions. If your garden is predominately a woodland site, focus on longer sweeps of shade-tolerant plants like ferns and sweet fern, a small shrub. If all or some stretches of your path bask in the sunshine for at least four to six hours, plant masses of lavender and basil.

- Include upright grasses and sages for vertical accents and four-season interest.

- Soften the edges of the path with low-growing plants like peppermint geranium and ornamental oregano.

- Strike a balance between spontaneity and formality by allowing self-sowing annuals such as fern-leaf lavender, holy basil, and even tomatoes to reseed freely. Then edit at leisure.

- Clip back or transplant plants that spring up between the paving stones, or leave them be for a somewhat wilder, more informal look.

## Plants Featured in This Garden

For a printer-friendly garden plan drawn to scale, go to bbg.org/fragrantdesigns.

1 *Anthemis nobilis,* chamomile

2 *Berlandiera lyrata,* chocolate flower

3 *Comptonia peregrina,* sweet fern

4 *Dennstaedtia punctilobula,* hay-scented fern

5 *Lavandula multifida,* fern-leaf lavender

6 *Lycopersicon esculentum,* tomato

7 *Ocimum sanctum* (syn. *O. tenuiflorum*), holy basil, tulsi

8 *Origanum laevigatum,* ornamental oregano

9 *Pelargonium tomentosum,* peppermint geranium

10 *Perovskia atriplicifolia,* Russian sage

11 *Salvia sclarea,* clary sage

12 *Sporobolus heterolepis,* prairie dropseed

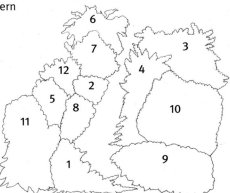

# Plants for a Scented Path

*With the exception of a few prairie plants that need full sun, the plants chosen to border this path are highly adaptable woodland natives that tolerate a wide range of light, soil, and moisture conditions.*

## Anthemis nobilis | Chamomile
**Mat-forming perennial; 12 inches tall**

Chamomile is the quintessential fragrant path plant. A mat-forming perennial with aromatic, finely divided leaves to 2 inches long and long-stalked, solitary flowers with yellow disks and creamy-white ray florets that appear in summer, chamomile is a lovely herb, on its own or in combination with other plants. Whether lining a path, planted between steppingstones, or in a container, chamomile is garden-worthy for its fragrant lacy foliage, and it makes a show when in bloom. Native to Europe, chamomile has naturalized throughout the U.S. All parts of the plant possess a fruity, apple fragrance.

**Growing Tips** You'll be most successful with chamomile if you establish plants early in the growing season and avoid heavy foot traffic right after planting. This native of areas with cool, wet summers needs to be well watered on hot days; planting it in a spot that receives a little midday shade will help. Chamomile does best in well-drained, slightly sandy soil. Clip the flower heads to direct the plant's energy toward root formation. In a spot that suits its needs, chamomile will spread, gradually filling in gaps and knitting together to form a weed-smothering mat. Zones 5 to 9.

**Alternatives** *Anthemis nobilis* 'Flore pleno' is a double-flowered chamomile. 'Treneague' is a nonflowering cultivar, recommended for lawns or paths. Its nonflowering habit keeps it tidy and eliminates the need for clipping or mowing. American pennyroyal (*Hedeoma pulegioides*) is a bushy native annual with minty foliage. Corsican mint (*Mentha requienii*) is a diminutive, mat-forming perennial resembling a moss but with a strong crème de menthe fragrance when brushed even lightly.

## Berlandiera lyrata
### Chocolate Flower
**Prairie perennial; 18 to 24 inches tall**

The chocolate flower, a prairie plant native to the U.S. Southwest, has felted gray-green leaves and light yellow, daisy-type flowers whose unique characteristics invite close and detailed observation. The flower's underside has chocolate-red striations; the flower buds and seed heads are remarkably symmetrical. Its chocolate fragrance is strongest and most mouthwatering in early morning. Chocolate flower blooms profusely from midsummer through fall.

**Growing Tips** As with many drought-tolerant prairie natives, this plant needs

***Berlandiera lyrata*, chocolate flower**

**_Dennstaedtia punctilobula_, hay-scented fern**

protection from excessive water, especially during its dormancy. A site that drains quickly and gets plenty of sun is best. Pinch back and deadhead frequently to prolong the season of bloom, but leave some of the spent flowers at the end of the season to enjoy the ornamental seed heads. Zones 4 to 10.

**Alternatives** Spotted bee balm (_Monarda punctata_) is a fragrant native prairie plant with conspicuous pinkish-purple bracts over yellow flowers with purple spots in summer and fall and anise-scented foliage. Aromatic aster (_Symphyotrichum oblongifolium_, syn. _Aster oblongifolius_) has a mild minty fragrance. Simply pinch it back in midseason for a great end-of-season display.

## _Comptonia peregrina_
### Sweet Fern
Shrub; 4 feet tall

Despite its common name, this is not a fern but a woodland shrub with fernlike foliage. It releases a pungent, peppery scent that permeates the afternoon air. Native to the coastal regions of eastern North America, sweet fern's woodland fragrance is bound to make it a nature lover's favorite. Native Americans valued this plant as a poultice for toothache and a wash for poison ivy rash. Herbalists cut and dry the leaves in early summer for infusions. Plant sweet fern in a mass to best appreciate its fragrance.

**Growing Tips** Sweet fern prefers well-drained acidic soil in sun or partial shade. It can tolerate drought but needs adequate moisture to thrive. Zones 4 to 8.

**Alternatives** Native bayberry (_Myrica pensylvanica_) is an upright suckering shrub, tolerant of a wide range of conditions. With glossy evergreen foliage and a peppery, foliar fragrance, bayberry lends itself well to naturalistic landscapes. Virginia sweetspire (_Itea virginica_) is another easy native, with fragrant bottlebrush flowers in spring; it turns a deep crimson in fall.

## _Dennstaedtia punctilobula_
### Hay-Scented Fern
Perennial; 2 feet tall

Hay-scented fern is a common North American native with arching, delicate fronds. Most common in woodland settings,

*Lavandula multifida*, fern-leaf lavender

it is an opportunistic colonizer, readily establishing a dense stand in nearly any spot. It spreads rapidly and easily fills out challenging sites such as dry shade and grows in poor soil where little else will flourish. The plant emits a haylike scent noticeable when you brush against it or pass by a large stand. This lovely lime-green fern is quick to emerge in spring, its delicate fronds belying its durable nature.

**Growing Tips** Thriving in shade or full sun, hay-scented fern can handle extreme drought, distinguishing it from most other ferns, which scorch with too much sun and too little moisture. Easily propagated by rhizome division, the plant benefits from a light, annual topdressing of manure or compost. Zones 3 to 8.

**Alternatives** Foamflower (*Tiarella cordifolia*) is a native herbaceous, spreading groundcover with slightly vanilla-scented flowers in spring. It prefers a shaded, moist location. Native Allegheny spurge (*Pachysandra procumbens*) is a well-behaved groundcover with handsome mottled leaves that remain through the winter and die back in spring as lightly scented flowers emerge.

## Lavandula multifida
## Fern-Leaf Lavender

**Tender perennial, often grown as annual; 2 feet tall**

Fern-leaf lavender has feathery silver-green leaves and prolific violet-blue flowers borne throughout the summer on slender-branched spikes. In the heat of the day, it fills the air with a spicy, oregano-like scent. This lavender flowers in its first year from seed, making it an invaluable addition to the annual border and in regions where lavender has difficulty surviving the winter. Like other lavenders, this tender perennial can grow into a shrub in its native Mediterranean climate. In colder areas it produces abundant seeds and freely sows itself throughout the garden. Delicate, fernlike seedlings emerge in early summer from unexpected nooks, their silvery leaves distinguishing them from other plants even when tiny.

**Growing Tips** Fern-leaf lavender is easy to cultivate from seed and stands up to a variety of weather conditions. Start seeds indoors several weeks before the last frost and transplant once the soil has warmed. Pinch the stems back when it begins to flower to encourage strong branching and a profusion of showy flowers. It will tolerate drought along with high moisture and humidity. Zones 8 to 11.

**Alternatives** *Lavandula multifida* 'Spanish Eyes' is a little more compact and earlier flowering.

## *Lycopersicon esculentum*
## Tomato
**Tender perennial, often grown as annual; 6 feet tall**

The tomato is not a typical choice for a decorative landscape and it is frequently overlooked when gardeners choose fragrant plants. But tomato foliage has a powerful warm, savory fragrance that has significant and specific connotations: It is the universal smell of summer. While tomatoes may be somewhat demanding culturally, they have a natural sprawling habit that reaches out and engages the visitor. One thing is certain: If you plant a tomato, you will be sure to have volunteer seedlings year after year.

**Growing Tips** You can contain tomato plants by simply dropping a wire basket over them and weaving the wandering shoots in between the stays. Or your trellising can be a work of art: Tomatoes look particularly elegant draped around steel spirals, an easy, natural form for training this typically rangy plant. Train the tomato as a single stem, pinching its side shoots, but leave as many leaves as possible, because the sugar content of the fruit is directly correlated to the plant's capacity for photosynthesis. Zones 9 to 10.

**Alternatives** *Lycopersicon esculentum* 'Black Prince' is a Russian heirloom with deep purple-black fruit. 'Green Zebra' is a popular heirloom tomato with chartreuse and lime-green stripes. Currant tomato (*L. pimpinellifolium*) is a prolific vining plant.

## *Ocimum sanctum*
## (syn *O. tenuiflorum*)
## Holy Basil, Tulsi
**Annual; 2 to 3 feet tall**

Holy basil possesses a pungent licorice scent in all its parts and has purple or green-leafed cultivars that are as decorative, rewarding— and forgiving—as its relative sweet basil (*Ocimum basilicum*). It has been cultivated in India and Southeast Asia since antiquity, where it is revered for its medicinal and culinary qualities.

**Growing Tips** Even the novice gardener can successfully grow basil from seed started in spring. Holy basil is a frequent self-seeder. Weed carefully to promote self-sown seedlings emerging from unexpected but welcome nooks. Pinch back as you would sweet basil to stimulate stronger growth and lateral branching.

**Alternatives** *Ocimum sanctum* 'Purple' is a selection with darker purple leaves. Several of the Thai basils resemble holy basil but differ in fragrance and taste; *O. basilicum* 'Siam Queen' is especially attractive.

*Lycopersicon esculentum*, **tomato**

## Origanum laevigatum
### Ornamental Oregano
Perennial; 2 feet tall

This showy, graceful-looking perennial blooms mid- to late summer with a profusion of arching purple to rose bracts. The neat, small leaves contrast nicely with its stems of reddish purple. Though not used as commonly for a seasoning as sweet marjoram (*Origanum majorana*) or oregano (*O. vulgare*), ornamental oregano possesses the same distinctive fragrance and can be used as you would its more celebrated culinary cousins. In the garden, the scent is most noticeable in the heat of day. Planting it close to heat-collecting stonework helps spread its fragrance.

**Growing Tips** All oreganos require good drainage. They look great in spots that suit their cascading habits—over a path, a wall, or the edge of a container. Zones 6 to 10.

**Alternatives** *Origanum laevigatum* 'Herrenhausen' has larger flower bracts than the species. 'Hopleys Purple' blooms profusely. 'Silver Anniversary' is a variegated form with white margins on the leaves.

Dittany of Crete (*O. dictamnus*) is an extremely worthy garden plant with a long history of medicinal, culinary, and ritualistic uses. Kent's dittany (*O.* 'Kent's Beauty') is a common and highly aromatic hybrid.

## Pelargonium tomentosum
### Peppermint Geranium
Tender perennial, often grown as annual; 18 to 24 inches tall

Peppermint geranium has soft downy leaves reminiscent of lamb's ear in texture, but a deeper shade of green. The palmate leaves hold the morning dew, giving the plant an iridescent, silvery appearance. A low-growing spreader with peppermint-stick fragrance, peppermint geranium looks equally attractive creeping across the ground or cascading over a ledge.

**Growing Tips** Allow scented geraniums to stay on the dry side to encourage the release of their fragrant oil. These South African natives cannot tolerate frost. They are easily propagated by softwood cuttings taken in late summer or winter, or you can cut the plant back, dig it up, and overwinter it as a houseplant. Zones 9 to 10.

**Alternatives** Nutmeg-scented geranium (*Pelargonium fragrans,* page 83) has a spicy fragrance, smaller silver-green leaves, and rose-tinged white flowers.

## Perovskia atriplicifolia
### Russian Sage
Perennial; 4 to 5 feet tall

Russian sage, an old favorite and reliable perennial, has silver stems and foliage and spikes of pale purple-blue flowers in mid-summer through fall. It adds a silvery, translucent effect to the garden and looks great in combination with almost any other plant. It releases a rich, spicy, sagelike aroma when you brush it. Plants can be grown alone as specimens or massed for a dramatic effect.

*Salvia sclarea,* **Clary Sage**

*Perovskia atriplicifolia,* **Russian sage**

**Growing Tips** Russian sage is a forgiving shrublike perennial that thrives in hot, humid weather and is extremely drought tolerant, but excessive winter moisture can cause root rot. Leave it alone for winter interest, or for more uniform growth, prune it to the ground in fall. It is easy to propagate, as it sends out multiple offshoots. Zones 5 to 9.

**Alternatives** *Perovskia atriplicifolia* 'Little Spire' offers more compact growth and 'Filigran' more dissected foliage. Southernwood (*Artemisia abrotanum*) has a similar effect in the garden and releases a pine scent when lightly brushed.

## *Salvia sclarea* | Clary Sage
Biennial; 3 feet tall

Unlike many other sages, clary sage has scented flowers as well as foliage. Its scent is described as both grapefruity and sagelike. A biennial, it produces a handsome rosette of downy silver leaves in its first year and a flower spike 3 or more feet tall the following year. A dominant plant in flower, clary sage serves as a great focal point for any garden composition.

**Growing Tips** Clary sage can tolerate heat and drought, but rich soil and adequate water are rewarded with fuller bloom. Transplant first-year seedlings of this reliable self-seeder to spots where you would like them to flower the second year. Do not use this plant in Washington State, where it is classified as a noxious weed. Zones 5 to 9.

**Alternatives** *Salvia sclarea* 'Turkestanica' has larger floral bracts than the species, and with its contrasting bracts of lavender and lilac pink, it is incredibly showy in combination with the cultivar 'Alba', which has white flowers, and yarrow (*Achillea millefolium*), also white flowered. Many California-native sages have a mild rosemary fragrance. Try musk sage (*S. clevelandii*), with blue flowers, hardy to Zone 8, or mountain desert sage (*S. pachyphylla*), Zones 6 to 9.

## *Sporobolus heterolepis*
## Prairie Dropseed
Prairie grass; 18 to 24 inches tall and wide

See page 40.

# Fragrant Rose Gardens

## Anne O'Neill

This simple sustainable rose garden has fragrance as its central theme. It shows, in broad strokes, how to combine various types of roses and a range of other fragrant plants in a modern setting. It features vigorous and moderate climbers, modern shrub roses, and species roses, setting them off against a display of evergreens, deciduous shrubs, perennials, groundcovers, and bulbs.

Roses are divided into many groups, and trying to understand the various classifications can be quite an undertaking. For a gardener, it is often easiest to find the right rose for a spot based on its garden characteristics. Start by considering the plant shape and size that you need and the flower color you would like, and then find these attributes combined in a rose that is disease resistant and hardy in your climate. For more in-depth information, check the rose resources at bbg.org/fragrantdesigns.

The selection of companion plants in this design provides structure, form, texture, seasonal succession, fragrance, and color for a rose garden that looks and smells great from early spring to late fall. The supporting cast of plants chosen for this project looks particularly well with roses, showcasing the roses' strengths and distracting from their weaknesses.

The primary structural plants include the narrowly upright *Taxus* × *media* 'Flushing', a lovely slow-growing, hardy yew cultivar, and the witch-hazel *Hamamelis* × *intermedia* 'Angelly', a beautiful small tree with fragrant early-spring flowers and good foliage color. Lily-of-the-valley, *Convallaria*, massed under the witch-hazel near the door, is fragrant early in the year, enticing people out on sunny days in early spring. Small spring bulbs planted in drifts throughout the garden lend fragrant support. Woodland strawberry, *Fragaria vesca*, scattered as a groundcover through the rest of the garden, is sturdy enough to be walked on occasionally for maintaining the garden and getting up close to appreciate the fragrance of the roses and their companions.

**A fertile bed that has good drainage and receives at least six hours of sunlight per day is ideal for combining roses with a range of other scented plants, such as clematis.**

# A Small Fragrant Rose Garden

# Roses Featured in This Garden

The illustration at left shows a partial view of the garden. For a printer-friendly plan of the entire garden, visit bbg.org/fragrantdesigns.

1 *Rosa alba* 'Great Maiden's Blush'

2 *Rosa* 'Cecile Brunner' (not pictured)

3 *Rosa* 'Climbing Westerland' (not pictured)

4 *Rosa* 'Compassion'

5 *Rosa* 'Dublin Bay'

6 *Rosa* 'Graham Thomas'

7 *Rosa* 'Julia Child'

8 *Rosa* 'Madame Hardy' (not pictured)

9 *Rosa* 'Paul McCartney' (not pictured)

10 *Rosa* × *primula*, incense rose (not pictured)

11 *Rosa* 'Stanwell Perpetual'

12 *Rosa* 'Sombreuil'

## Companion Plants

A *Clematis armandii,* Armand's clematis

B *Clematis* 'Evisix' (PETIT FAUCON)

C *Clematis recta* subsp. *purpurea,* ground clematis

D *Clethra alnifolia* 'Ruby Spire', summersweet

E *Convallaria majalis,* lily-of-the-valley (not pictured)

F *Foeniculum vulgare,* bronze fennel

G *Fragaria vesca,* woodland strawberry

H *Gardenia augusta* 'Chuck Hayes', hardy gardenia (not pictured)

I *Geranium* 'Roxanne', hardy geranium (not pictured)

J *Hamamelis* × *intermedia* 'Angelly', witch-hazel (not pictured)

K *Lilium formosanum,* Formosa lily

L *Taxus* × *media* 'Flushing', yew

M *Teucrium chamaedrys,* germander (not pictured)

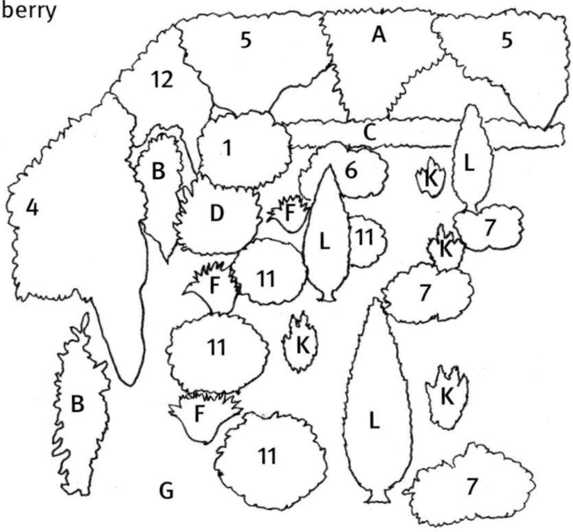

## Spring-Flowering Bulbs

Small bulbs (not pictured) that flower at different times in spring are planted in drifts throughout the garden. By the time the roses bloom, they have all retreated underground.

*Hyacinthus* 'Anastacia'

*Iris reticulata* 'Pixie'

*Muscari macrocarpum* 'Golden Fragrance'

*Narcissus* 'Beautiful Eyes' and 'Sundial'

*Narcissus poeticus* var. *recurvus*

*Rosa × primula*, **incense rose**

## ROSE CULTIVATION TIPS

- Roses need fertile, well-drained soil, as do many garden plants. You can increase the organic matter content in your soil by adding well-rotted manure and compost. Improve its mineral content with greensand, which also bolsters biological activity, water retention, and fertility. If your soil is heavy, poorly draining clay, add coarse sand, chicken grit, and organic matter before planting roses. Amend sandy soil with organic matter and greensand. Garden roses (except *Rosa rugosa* species and cultivars, which have shown to be invasive in coastal dune areas) will fail during summer heat in unamended sandy soil.

- Mulching is essential for roses. After winter has settled in New York in January, I put an active mulch such as spent mushroom compost or Sweet Peet around the roses, then lay additional cover such as pine branches on some of the less robust plants. In March, I spread out the mulch and prune. In April, I top-dress the beds with a little additional mulch. In early spring, the mulch reduces weed seed germination, maintains moisture levels, and protects the soil from heavy rains. Perennials gradually grow in around the roses, protecting the plants and soil during high summer and autumn. The mulch gradually breaks down, improving the soil throughout the year.

- Roses do not like wet feet or leaves. In poorly drained soil, their roots are more likely to be attacked by pathogens. The leaves of roses will stay essentially free of fungal attack if they are dry. In humid climates, where this is difficult to accomplish, choose disease-resistant plants. Water your soil as infrequently as practical (let it dry to at least one inch below the surface), then drench it deeply very early in the morning to avoid excessive evaporation and to allow your plants to dry before the sun gets high. Make sure there's adequate room around plants for good air circulation.

# Fragrant Roses

*The 12 roses profiled here are all easy to grow in many regions, including the Northeast, and all will be essentially healthy in any place with fertile soil, good drainage and air circulation, and at least six hours of direct sunlight. For best success, gardeners in the South should lean toward tea roses, noisettes, and other roses that bloom through the longer season of heat and respond well to the easier winters. Gardeners in Minnesota, Maine, and other regions with severe winter weather and relatively short summers should choose tough, resilient plants (preferably those growing on their own roots rather than on grafted rootstock) that recover quickly in spring and are ready for dormancy again in autumn. Roses developed by Dr. Griffith Bucks are wonderful for these colder regions, as are Kordes, Canadian series, and Gallica roses and many of the old garden roses.*

## Shrub Roses

### *Rosa alba* 'Great Maiden's Blush'
**Shrub; 8 feet tall and 5 wide**

'Great Maiden's Blush' has been grown since before the 15th century and was particularly popular in monasteries. The leaves are slate blue, and the late-spring flowers are an intoxicating profusion of blush-pink perfection with a light scent that lingers in the air. An arching habit and blue leaves make 'Great Maiden's Blush' attractive through the seasons. It is tough!

### *Rosa* 'Cecile Brunner'
**Shrub; 4 feet tall and 2 feet wide**

This is a little rose with a big heart. However it is classified, it is a great garden plant, with long, elegant leaves on smooth, thin green stems and sprays of small blush-colored, perfectly formed fragrant blooms held above a healthy but delicately formed little rosebush. Throughout the season it just keeps blooming.

### *Rosa* 'Graham Thomas'
**Shrub; 5 feet tall and 3 feet wide**

Introduced by English rose breeder David Austin, this rose has wonderful golden-yellow, old-style blooms with strong fragrance. In New York, it tends to be at its best

in fall, with incredibly generous flowering right into late November. It is a bit leggy and usually looks better when planted in a group of three, which gives it some heft to go with its height. In warmer-winter areas, this rose can grow much taller.

### *Rosa* 'Julia Child'
**Rounded shrub; 3½ feet tall and wide**

This disease-resistant modern floribunda rose, bred by Tom Carruth of Weeks Roses, has a neat habit and glossy, healthy-looking leaves and generous, consistent blooms throughout the season. It was chosen by the

*Rosa* 'Graham Thomas'

*Rosa* 'Madame Hardy'

chef and cookbook author Julia Child for its buttery-yellow, open flowers and strong, spicy fragrance. I like this rose planted in small informal groups, usually about three plants, within olfactory reach of everybody using the garden.

### *Rosa* 'Madame Hardy'
Shrub; 6 feet tall and 5 feet wide

This classic old garden rose is a damask with elegant growth and unforgettable flowers. The heavily fragrant blossoms are double white with a green eye showing through. This easy shrub in also useful as background greenery during the summer and autumn, and its canes add structure during the winter months. It is a beautiful plant, particularly when planted with complementary perennials.

### *Rosa* 'Paul McCartney'
Shrub; up to 8 feet tall and 3 feet wide

This rose is classified as a hybrid tea in the U.S. It grows like the most vigorous of modern shrubs and is very robust and floriferous. It has strong-stemmed, large pink

blooms with classic hybrid tea form—a high center. The fragrance is amazing, lingering to fill the evening air. It is a great newer rose that thrives with only a minimum of care and justifies its place in most gardens. It may grow to 8 feet in warmer-winter areas.

### *Rosa* × *primula*
### Incense Rose
Shrub; 6 feet tall and 5 feet wide

This wonderful garden shrub is a hybrid species rose from Asia with shiny, pinnate leaves on a small, well-behaved, and quite lovely vase-shaped plant that looks handsome even in winter. The foliage has a spicy scent that's especially strong after a rain. Incense rose is covered in single yellow fragrant flowers in mid spring. It leaves the ever popular forsythia in the dust!

### *Rosa* 'Stanwell Perpetual'
Shrub; 6 feet tall and 5 feet wide

'Stanwell Perpetual' is a prickly, arching shrub with fairly thin reddish canes and blue-tinged leaves. It is a tough, hardy, and disease-resistant plant, with recurrent fully double, quartered, soft blush-pink blossoms. The lovely fragrance is described as wild rose but heady, which is explained by its parentage. Introduced in the U.K. in 1838, it is reported to be a cross between a burnet rose (*R. pimpinellifolia*) and a damask (*R. × damascena*).

## Climbing Roses

### Rosa 'Climbing Westerland'
Climber; up to 12 feet tall

This large-flowered climber blooms well throughout the growing season. It has large, shiny dark green foliage and very fragrant flowers in a yellow-peach-orange blend on a relatively small climbing plant. It is ideal on arbors, particularly in the Northeast. It has great disease resistance.

### Rosa 'Compassion'
Climber; up to 15 feet tall

This vigorous climber has large-flowered, shapely, high-centered scented flowers of apricot, copper, and yellow with pink shading—which despite the description do not clash. The leaves are a dark glossy green. The plant is strong, and it blooms semicontinuously from June through November. Is it any surprise that the rose is our national flower?

### Rosa 'Dublin Bay'
Climber; up to 12 feet tall

'Dublin Bay' has glossy leaves and large, sweetly scented dark red flowers. It has consistently been chosen as the best red climber in the Northeast.

### Rosa 'Sombreuil'
Climber; up to 12 feet tall

This large-flowered rose has very fragrant, creamy-white flowers. It is a gentle climber and may get a little winter damage in the Northeast, but it is a must-have plant due to the beauty of its habit, its good health, and the fragrance of its lovely recurrent blooms.

**Rosa 'Dublin Bay'**

# Architectural Plants for the Rose Garden

*Taxus* × *media* 'Flushing' A fastigiate, or narrowly upright, yew was chosen for its historical association with rose gardens. 'Flushing' has strong shape and color, grows to 10 feet tall and 2 feet wide, and does well in most gardens. Zones 4 to 7.

*Hamamelis* × *intermedia* 'Angelly' This witch-hazel has a long season of interest, spicily fragrant bright yellow early-spring flowers, dark early foliage, and orange autumn colors. It is a compact selection that works well in a smaller garden, reaching 6 to 6½ feet. Zones 5 to 8. (See pages 30 and 49 for larger witch-hazels.)

*Clematis* species and cultivars With their gracefully twining habit, exuberant velvety flowers, and eye-catching seedpods that often look like tufty swirling mop heads, clematis vines make great rose companions. Armand's clematis, *Clematis armandii*, grows up and over the sun-warmed back wall. Hardy in Zones 7 to 9, it is a little tender for New York City where I garden, but it usually survives on a southwest-facing wall. It is worthwhile because it is extremely fragrant, grows vigorously, and has beautiful evergreen leaves. The smaller *Clematis* 'Evisix' (PETIT FAUCON) clambers over the side fences. Zones 4 to 9. Nonvining ground clematis, *Clematis recta* subsp. *purpurea*, is used as a groundcover. It has purple leaves and fragrant white flowers. Zones 3 to 9.

*Foeniculum vulgare* Growing to 5 feet tall, bronze fennel adds color, texture, structure, height, and movement. It self-seeds and transplants easily, making it an ideal structural plant for summer. Zones 4 to 9.

*Gardenia augusta* 'Chuck Hayes' This hardy gardenia cultivar is featured on either side of the patio (see full garden plan at bbg.org/fragrantdesigns). It blooms through summer and into late autumn, its fragrance wafting into the house through the open windows. Zones 7 to 9.

*Lilium formosanum* Formosa lily provides structure with its commanding 6-foot-tall flower stalks and gorgeous white, fragrant, trumpet-shaped flowers, which bloom in late summer through fall when the garden needs them most. Zones 5 to 9.

*Convallaria majalis*, lily-of-the-valley

## Groundcovers

*Convallaria majalis* Lily-of-the-valley has lovely light green leaves emerging in spring like a woodland carpet and beautiful fragrant spring flowers. Zones 3 to 7.

*Fragaria vesca* Gardeners have used woodland strawberry under roses for centuries. Some people find it quite fragrant, especially after rain. It can sustain occasional foot traffic. Zones 3 to 9.

*Geranium* 'Roxanne' This lovely blue-flowered hardy geranium blooms almost continuously from May through November. Its tidy procumbent (trailing) form makes it easy to use as a foil for roses. Zones 5 to 8.

**Fragaria vesca, woodland strawberry**

*Teucrium chamaedrys* This low-growing germander has small, glossy, evergreen aromatic leaves, is easily maintained, and responds well to shearing. It has pretty pink flowers in June and July. Zones 4 to 9.

## Spring-Flowering Bulbs

Plant these bulbs in drifts throughout the garden, setting them out in casual groups of a dozen or more. If that sounds like an awful lot of bulb planting, start with one or two. Check for noticeable bald spots in spring, and add a few more bulbs each fall.

*Hyacinthus* 'Anastacia' This old-fashioned hyacinth bears light purple flowers in early to mid-spring; 6 to 12 inches tall; Zones 4 to 8.

*Iris reticulata* 'Pixie' The deep blue flowers of this reticulated iris appear in early spring; 4 to 6 inches tall; Zones 3 to 9.

*Muscari macrocarpum* 'Golden Fragrance' This grape hyacinth has yellow florets with a purple crown in mid- to late spring; 5 to 8 inches tall; Zones 4 to 9.

*Narcissus* 'Beautiful Eyes' A daffodil with creamy-white flowers with orange centers, it blooms in mid- to late spring; 12 to 24 inches tall; Zones 4 to 9.

*Narcissus* 'Sundial' Clusters of tiny yellow flowers with a green eye in late spring distinguish this daffodil; up to 12 inches tall; Zones 4 to 9.

*Narcissus poeticus* var. *recurvus* This daffodil bears white flowers with strongly recurved petals and a yellow cup in late spring; to 12 inches tall; Zones 3 to 7.

*Schizophragma hydrangeoides*, Japanese hydrangea vine

# Fragrant Annual and Perennial Vines
## Andrew Bunting

It is hard to imagine a fragrance garden without a vine. Some of the most highly scented plants ever used by gardeners have been vines—Chinese wisteria (*Wisteria sinensis*), Japanese wisteria (*W. floribunda*), Japanese honeysuckle (*Lonicera japonica*), and sweet autumn clematis (*Clematis terniflora*) are just a few of the better-known examples. Because of their weedy and invasive nature, though, these once-favored vines are no longer promoted as good plants for the home garden. However, many other outstanding vines provide wonderful fragrances and bloom throughout the growing season—among them different clematis species, woody vines, and annual and tropical vines that are readily available through mail-order sources and at garden centers.

Vines add drama to a garden. They turn walls, fences, trellises, and even containers into vertical garden spaces, bringing their blossoms up to nose level where they are best appreciated. They create a backdrop for the fragrant, ornamental companion plants—trees, shrubs, and perennials that are worked in around them. The vines featured here supply scent from early spring through October. All are very easy to grow. Most will grow best in full sun; however, climbing hydrangea (*Hydrangea petiolaris*), Japanese hydrangea vine (*Schizophragma hydrangeoides*), and cross vine (*Bignonia capreolata*) will grow fairly well in some shade. Consider incorporating a vine or two from this selection into the other fragrant garden designs in this book.

# TIPS FOR INTEGRATING VINES IN A GARDEN

- For gardeners with small spaces, vines are a great option. Apartment dwellers can grow vines in pots on their balconies and up and around windows.

- Complement permanent, perennial vines with annual vines. I sometimes plant one at the base of a woody or perennial vine, which serves as a living trellis.

- Plant scented vines around windows and doors so their fragrance floats in on the breeze.

- Combine vines with other plants of contrasting foliage. For example, the finely textured yellow-green leaves of *Jasminum officinale* 'Frojas' (FIONA SUNRISE), grown up through the dissected foliage of a Japanese maple such as *Acer palmatum* 'Crimson Queen', creates a stunning chartreuse-burgundy combination.

## *Actinidia kolomikta* | Hardy Kiwi
Twining perennial; 15 to 25 feet tall

Hardy kiwi vine is grown first and foremost for its stunning foliage. As they emerge in spring, the leaves are variegated white and green with pink tips, making them look as if a housepainter inadvertently splattered them. As the season progresses and the intensity of light increases, most of this coloration fades. Under the foliage in May, the vine bears tiny clusters of fragrant white flowers. Hardy kiwi bears delicious fruits as long as you have both a male and female plant in proximity. Male plants have better leaf color.

**Growing Tips** This twining vine, native to coniferous forests in Japan, China, and Korea, thrives in a well-drained soil in full sun. It needs some sort of trellising or arbor for support. Zones 4 to 8.

## *Bignonia capreolata* | Cross Vine
Perennial vine; 60 feet tall

This vine native to the Southeast attaches itself to a surface by sending out delicate tendrils whose tips find their way into the tiniest of crevices and then swell to seal themselves tight. This seemingly precarious method of attachment enables cross vine to grow up to 60 feet tall and fully support itself. From May to June, it bears 2-inch-long, sweetly fragrant orange tubular flowers. In protected locations and in southern gardens, *Bignonia* can be semievergreen to

**Bignonia capreolata, cross vine**

evergreen. In northern climates, the glossy leaves turn a beautiful purplish hue in fall.

**Growing Tips** For best flowering, plant this drought-tolerant vine in full sun. Zones 6 to 9.

## *Clematis montana* var. *rubens*
## Anemone Clematis
Perennial vine; 40 to 50 feet tall

In May this vine produces 2½-inch-wide flowers slightly scented with a hint of chocolate. The showy parts of the flowers are the four soft pink tepals; at their centers are tiny creamy flowers. The small, oval, serrated leaves emerge at the same time as the flowers.

**Growing Tips** Grow this very vigorous species from China in groups. You can use it to cover a chain-link fence, drape it over a rock pile, or let it clamber up a building. For best flowering, grow it in full sun. Wait to prune until after flowering in the spring, since it flowers relatively early. Zones 4 to 9.

### *Decumaria barbara*
### Wood Vamp
Perennial vine; 10 to 20 feet tall

One of my favorite fragrant native vines is the wood vamp, or wild hydrangea vine, which comes from swamps and bottomland forests of the coastal plains of Virginia and points south. For the native garden, the wood vamp is a great choice for growing up the trunk of a tree. I grow this self-clinging vine (attaching by rootlets along the stem) on the east side of my stone house, where it thrives. From late June to early July, wood vamp is covered in tight clusters of tiny yellowish-white, very fragrant flowers. These have a fresh, grassy scent and are a nectar source for butterflies, including swallowtails. The lustrous dark green leaves are attractive throughout the growing season and turn a beautiful butter yellow in the autumn.

**Growing Tips** Wood vamp grows well in full sun to almost full shade and prefers a slightly moist soil. Zones 5 to 9.

### *Dregea* (syn. *Wattakaka*) *sinensis* | Wattakaka Vine
Tender perennial vine; 10 feet tall

From May to July, this twining vine is loaded with open-faced hanging panicles of waxy, starlike flowers with a sweet, heavy, musky fragrance. Each flower cluster has at least a dozen white flowers, each with a soft lavender center. The leaves are heart-shaped and sometimes variegated. Wattakaka vine is hardy in the southern states and California; otherwise it is grown as an annual.

**Growing Tips** For the best floral display and to take full advantage of its heady fragrance, grow this vine on a tripod in a terracotta pot or other decorative container on a patio, terrace, or balcony. The container should be a minimum of 18 inches in diameter and filled with a well-draining potting soil. Fertilize every two weeks with a balanced fertilizer (NPK 20-20-20 or similar) to encourage luxuriant growth and an abundance of flowering. Zones 10 to 11.

### *Gelsemium sempervirens*
### Carolina Jessamine
Perennial vine; 15 feet tall or more

See page 48.

### *Hydrangea petiolaris*
### Climbing Hydrangea
Perennial vine or groundcover; 30 to 50 feet tall

Long a popular fragrant vine for shady locations, this self-clinging vine native to Japan and China flowers in July, with a sweet fragrance. At the center of each 6- to 10-inch lacecap flower head are tiny white fertile flowers surrounded by a ring of showier, white, four-parted sterile flowers resembling four-leaf clovers. The inflorescences last two

*Clematis montana* var. *rubens*, anemone clematis

weeks, filling the garden with fragrance. Climbing hydrangea's rounded leaves turn golden in fall.

**Growing Tips** Though it will thrive in both sun and shade, climbing hydrangea flowers best in dappled shade. Gardeners often ask me why their climbing hydrangeas are not blooming. The most likely reason is that the vine is too young—it can sometimes take seven years to flower. Zones 4 to 8.

## *Jasminum officinale* 'Frojas'
### (FIONA SUNRISE) | Poet's Jasmine
Tender perennial vine; 30 to 40 feet tall

This is a relatively new selection of the common white jasmine. Like the species, it produces clusters of intensely lemon-scented, white star-shaped flowers from June through October, but it is slower growing and has striking chartreuse foliage. Flowering occurs better and more prolifically in southern regions. In the garden it is lovely clambering over low stone walls or intertwined with the foliage of small trees or shrubs with contrasting leaf color.

**Growing Tips** *Jasminum officinale* is listed as a Zone 8 plant, but this selection has been successfully overwintered in Swarthmore, Pennsylvania (Zone 7). For the best foliage color and flowering, plant it in full sun. Zones 7 to 10.

## *Lonicera × heckrottii*
### Goldflame Honeysuckle
Perennial vine; 10 to 13 feet tall

A good substitute for the highly invasive Japanese honeysuckle (*Lonicera japonica*), goldflame honeysuckle is not as fragrant, but its floral display is perhaps the best of all the climbing honeysuckles. The tubular flower buds, deep pinkish red, emerge in May, then open to reveal an inner tube of white and yellow. As more flowers open, the vine becomes a festive mosaic of pink, white, and yellow. Many climbing honeysuckles flower for a finite period, but *L. × heckrottii*

**_Lonicera × heckrottii_, goldflame honeysuckle**

continues blooming sporadically, wafting its fragrance throughout the summer. Goldflame honeysuckle, a hybrid between *L. sempervirens* and *L. × americana*, is one of the best fragrant vines for attracting hummingbirds to the garden.

**Growing Tips** For optimal flowering, plant honeysuckle in full sun in a soil rich in organic matter. It benefits from support, such as a split-rail fence or trellis. In spring the new foliage can be affected by aphids, but it usually outgrows this pest problem. After flowering, prune the vine lightly to prevent it from becoming a tangled mess. Zones 5 to 9.

## *Schizophragma hydrangeoides*
### Japanese Hydrangea Vine
Perennial vine; 30 feet tall

Among the most ornamental of all fragrant vines is the Japanese hydrangea vine, *Schizophragma hydrangeoides*, a native of Japan and Korea. This fantastic woody climber is self-clinging (but not destructive to mortar) and can make its way up fences, walls, and tree trunks. In late June to early July, it bears flat-topped flower clusters 6 to 8

inches across with a sweet, refreshing scent. These clusters of tiny white flowers are sparsely encircled by pale bracts that appear to hover suspended above the flowers. The sweetly fragrant, pure white blooms add a great deal of interest to the garden, particularly in the evening. The vine's large, serrated, heart-shaped leaves turn yellow in the autumn.

**Growing Tips** This vine grows best on an east- or north-facing wall or corner in slightly moist soil; the light exposure can range from sun to shade. Zones 5 to 8.

### *Trachelospermum jasminoides*
### Confederate or Star Jasmine
**Tender perennial vine; 40 feet tall**

The Confederate or star jasmine, the hallmark of fragrant vines in the South (though a native of China), is a twining evergreen vine or groundcover with small oval, leathery leaves. The five-petaled, inch-long white flowers tinged with yellow are borne in May to June. Flowering sporadically throughout the summer, this vine will benefit from a little judicious pruning

occasionally to keep it looking tidy. The sweet fragrance of the flowers is like that of an Oriental lily.

**Growing Tips** For the best flower display, train Confederate jasmine on a trellis, arbor, or fence. In the northern limit of its range, plant it where it will get some protection, such as in a courtyard. All parts of this plant are poisonous if ingested, and it can cause skin irritation or an allergic reaction when touched, so handle carefully. Zones 7 to 10.

### *Wisteria frutescens*
### American wisteria
**Perennial vine; 20 to 30 feet tall**

American wisteria, a native of moist or wet woods and riverbanks from Virginia to Louisiana, is a wonderful alternative to the weedy and aggressive Japanese and Chinese wisterias (although it is much less vigorous). Its flowers appear in June, much later than those of the Asian species, and they are not the familiar long dangling clusters of flowers but rather upright, stout cones 6 to 9 inches long. The pealike flowers are lavender with a yellow spot and have a sweet, fruity fragrance. American wisteria's foliage resembles that of the Asian species, with shiny, dark green compound leaves. I grow it on a rail fence, where it has extended about 15 feet. When it blooms, the lovely flowers completely cover the vine.

**Growing Tips** For best flowering, grow American wisteria in full sun. Zones 5 to 9.

***Wisteria frutescens*, American wisteria**

# Nursery Sources

The best way to judge the appeal of a scented plant is to actually smell it, so you may have the best luck finding plants that you love at a local nursery. But you'll find a much broader selection of fragrant plants and seeds through mail order and online sources.

**The Antique Rose Emporium**
9300 Lueckemeyer Road
Brenham, TX 77833
800-441-0002
www.antiqueroseemporium.com

**Brushwood Nursery**
247 E. Street Road
Kennett Square, PA 19348
610-444-8083
www.gardenvines.com

**Carroll Gardens**
444 East Main Street
Westminster, MD 21157
800-638-6334
www.carrollgardens.com

**Digging Dog Nursery**
P.O. Box 471
Albion, CA 95410
707-937-1130
www.diggingdog.com

**Fairweather Gardens**
P.O. Box 330
Greenwich, NJ 08323
856-451-6261
www.fairweathergardens.com

**Forest Farm Nursery**
990 Tetherow Road
Williams, OR 97544-9599
541-846-7269
www.forestfarm.com

**The Fragrant Path**
P.O. Box 328
Fort Calhoun, NE 68023
www.fragrantpathseeds.com

**High Country Gardens**
2902 Rufina Street
Santa Fe, NM 87507
800-925-9387
www.highcountrygardens.com

**J.L. Hudson, Seedsman**
P.O. Box 337
La Honda, CA 94020
www.jlhudsonseeds.net

**Las Pilitas Nursery**
3232 Las Pilitas Road
Santa Margarita, CA 93453
805-438-5992
www.laspilitas.com

**Logees Tropical Plants**
141 North Street
Danielson, CT 06239
888-330-8038
www.logees.com

**Niche Gardens**
1111 Dawson Road
Chapel Hill, NC 27516
919-967-0078
www.nichegardens.com

**Park Seed Company**
1 Parkton Avenue
Greenwood, SC 29647
800-213-0076

**Plant Delights**
9241 Sauls Road
Raleigh, NC 27603
919-772-4794
www.plantdelights.com

**Rare Find Nursery**
957 Patterson Road
Jackson, NJ 08527
732-833-0613
www.rarefindnursery.com

**Richters Herbs**
357 Highway 47
Goodwood, ON LoC 1Ao Canada
905-640-6677
www.richters.com

**Roses Unlimited**
363 North Deerwood Drive
Laurens, SC 29360
864-682-7673
rosesunlimitedownroot.com

**John Scheepers**
Kitchen Garden Seeds
23 Tulip Drive
P.O. Box 638
Bantam, CT 06750
860-567-6086
www.kitchengardenseeds.com

**Seed Savers Exchange**
3094 North Winn Road
Decorah, IA 52101
563-382-5990
www.seedsavers.org

**Select Seeds**
180 Stickney Hill Road
Union, CT 06076
800-684-0395
www.selectseeds.com

**Stokes Tropicals**
4806 E. Old Spanish Trail
Jeanerette, LA 70544
866-478-2502
www.stokestropicals.com

**Vintage Roses**
535 Griswold Street, Suite 111-517
Detroit, MI 483226
vintageroses.com

**Well-Sweep Herb Farm**
205 Mount Bethel Road
Port Murray, NJ 07865
908-852-5390
www.wellsweep.com

**Yerba Buena Nursery**
19500 Skyline Blvd.
Woodside, CA 94062
650-851-1668
www.yerbabuenanursery.com

To locate reputable suppliers of native plants in your area, visit the Lady Bird Johnson Wildflower Center website at wildflower.org/suppliers.

# Books

*Meaningful Scents Around the World: Olfactory, Chemical, Biological, and Cultural Considerations*
Roman Kaiser
John Wiley & Sons, 2006

*A Natural History of the Senses*
Diane Ackerman
Knopf Publishing Group, 1991

*Perfume: The Story of a Murderer*
Patrick Süskind
Knopf Publishing Group, 1986 (hardcover)
Random House, 2001 (paperback)

*What the Nose Knows*
Avery Gilbert
Random House, 2008

# Contributors

**Andrew Bunting** has been curator at the Scott Arboretum of Swarthmore College since 1993. The arboretum focuses on ornamental collections of woody plants, including hollies, magnolias, rhododendrons, and ornamental vines. For many years he taught the certificate course on ornamental vines at Longwood Gardens. He also owns Fine Garden Creations, a garden-design and installation company started in 1992 and located in Swarthmore, Pennsylvania.

**Claire Hagen Dole** is the former publisher of *Butterfly Gardeners' Quarterly*. She edited the BBG handbook *The Butterfly Gardener's Guide* (2003) and contributed to the BBG handbook *Designing an Herb Garden* (2004). She lives in Seattle, Washington, and writes about wildlife gardening for numerous publications. Claire's own hell strip was featured in an HGTV segment on gardening in 2002.

**Caleb Leech** is curator of the Herb Garden and Hardy Fern Collection at Brooklyn Botanic Garden and former curator of BBG's Alice Recknagel Ireys Fragrance Garden. He has gardened almost all his life, in many different climates. He currently focuses on community gardens, shared landscapes, and the connections people feel with plants and place.

**Beth Hanson** is a former managing editor of Brooklyn Botanic Garden's handbook series and is editor of ten BBG handbooks, including *Buried Treasures: Tasty Tubers of the World*, *The Best Apples to Buy and Grow*, *Easy Compost*, and *Natural Disease Control*. She also contributed to *The Brooklyn Botanic Garden's Gardener's Desk Reference* (Henry Holt, 1998). She lives outside New York City, where she is a master gardener volunteer and writes about science and health for various publications.

**Monika Hannemann** is an urban horticulturist and educator. Until recently, she managed the horticulture and family education programs in BBG's Discovery Garden, an adventure garden for children and families. All the plants in her chapter were tested and approved by young visitors in the Discovery Garden. She also worked with children in New York City schools, helping them connect with plants through gardening and growing food. Monika is currently training to become a certified arborist in Maplewood, New Jersey, and continuing her work with children.

**Janet Marinelli** is a former director of Publications at Brooklyn Botanic Garden. She has written several books on sustainable landscape design and blogs about all things photosynthetic on her website, janetmarinelli.com. Her work has garnered numerous awards, including the American Horticultural Society's prestigious American Gardener Award for writing "that has made a significant contribution to horticulture" and the 2008 Trudy Farrand/John Strohm magazine writing award from the National Wildlife Federation.

**Leda Meredith** is an ethnobotanist and an instructor at Brooklyn Botanic Garden and the New York Botanical Garden. She is the author of *Botany, Ballet & Dinner from Scratch: A Memoir with Recipes* (Heliotrope Books, 2008), and the winner of Adelphi University's 2008 Teaching Excellence Award.

Anne O'Neill has gardened in Ireland, England, and New York. She is curator of the Shakespeare Garden, Alice Recknagel Ireys Fragrance Garden, and members of the Plant Family Collection at Brooklyn Botanic Garden. She also was curator of the Cranford Rose Garden from 2001 until 2008. She has a particular interest in sustainable horticultural practices.

Meghan Ray worked at Brooklyn Botanic Garden from 1994 until 2006 as curator of the Shakespeare Garden, Alice Recknagel Ireys Fragrance Garden, and the Rock Garden, among others. In 2006, she joined the University of California Botanical Garden at Berkeley, where she manages the South African and Palm and Cycad collections. She has a master's degree in garden history and landscape studies from the Bard Graduate Center in New York City and writes and teaches about horticulture and landscape history.

Jennifer Williams has worked at Brooklyn Botanic Garden for almost ten years as a gardener in the Steinhardt Conservatory and specializes in interior display and container design. She is a graduate of the University of Georgia, where she studied drawing and painting. Before joining BBG, she pursued a career in independent filmmaking.

## Photos

Laura Berman pages 13, 16, 20, 29, 31, 32 (and back cover), 39, 40, 46, 56, 57, 82, 85, 96, 100, 109

Rob Cardillo cover, pages 2, 9, 43, 50, 52, 63

David Cavagnaro pages 18, 26 (and back cover), 36, 37, 60, 70, 74, 80, 83, 92, 93, 102, 104, 108

Alan & Linda Detrick pages 19, 95

Bill Johnson pages 8, 14, 17, 38, 41, 49, 51, 66, 67, 81, 84, 110

Roman Kaiser pages 10, 11

Charles Mann pages 4, 23, 28, 58, 59, 75, 90, 107

Jerry Pavia pages 7, 27, 30, 47, 48, 61, 71, 76, 87, 91, 94, 101, 103, 105, 106

## Illustrations

Elizabeth Ennis

# Index

# PROVIDING EXPERT GARDENING ADVICE FOR OVER 60 YEARS

Join Brooklyn Botanic Garden as a Subscriber Member to receive our award-winning gardening handbooks delivered directly to you, plus *Plants & Gardens News* and privileges at many botanic gardens across the country. Visit bbg.org/subscribe for details.

## BROOKLYN BOTANIC GARDEN ALL-REGION GUIDES

World renowned for pioneering gardening information, Brooklyn Botanic Garden's award-winning guides provide practical advice in a compact format for gardeners in every region of North America. To order other fine titles, call 718-623-7286 or shop online at shop.bbg.org. For additional information about Brooklyn Botanic Garden, call 718-623-7200 or visit bbg.org.